The Mind
AND THE Stock Market

The Mind
AND Stock Market
THE

$ $

A PRIMER FOR A BEGINNING INVESTOR

$ $

STEPHEN H. ARCHER

iUniverse®

THE MIND AND THE STOCK MARKET
A PRIMER FOR A BEGINNING INVESTOR

iUniverse books may be ordered through booksellers or by contacting:

iUniverse
1663 Liberty Drive
Bloomington, IN 47403
www.iuniverse.com
1-800-Authors (1-800-288-4677)

ISBN: 978-1-5320-1980-7 (sc)
ISBN: 978-1-5320-1982-1 (hc)
ISBN: 978-1-5320-1981-4 (e)

Library of Congress Control Number: 2017906100

Print information available on the last page.

iUniverse rev. date: 5/5/2017

CONTENTS

PART TWO
Investing and the Economy

PART THREE
People and Their Investing Influence

PART FOUR
Some Errors of the Mind in Investing

PART FIVE
Some Common Investment Alternatives

PART SIX
Financial Management of Investments

$ $

PREFACE

$ $

I've centered my career around investing. I invested, I worked in the securities industry, I received a doctoral degree in finance, I taught investing to college students, and I coauthored many textbooks on finance. All through my career, I have been troubled by the great impact that the mind and its emotions have played in personal and family investment. Little is said in investment books about the tricks that the mind can play in investment decisions.

In November 2016, the surprising result of the presidential election resulted in a quick drop in stock prices followed by a quick advance. For example, suppose a Mr. Anderson and his wife, who were considering starting an investment nest egg for retirement, became afraid that they were being left behind. Their fear brought them to a decision to buy some shares immediately. They were afraid of missing out on the gold rush. That fear is a mental attitude. The mind just entered the investment decision.

There are many books about the stock market, but that is not the place to start. Too many investment decisions involve not just profits, prices, and dividends but also the emotions of the mind—fear, regret, and ego. Most books leave that part out.

The Mind and the Stock Market brings the beginning investor's attention to the broad scope of investing. Beginners should be aware of the many investment alternatives beyond the stock market. They should learn the impacts of the economy; the interaction of peoples' minds and the investing process; and some of the common errors of stock market buying and selling. This book is a complete primer about investing. This is the place to start.

$ $

CHAPTER 1

$ $

Introduction

The stock market can be a bit of a mystery. It can be a place where fortunes are made—consider Warren Buffet, Carl Icahn, J. P. Morgan, Boone Pickens, George Soros, and Jay Gould. But it certainly can also be where fortunes are lost—consider Lehman Bros., among others. Many, many people less famous than these have lost or gained, or lost and then gained, or gained and lost again, and so on.

Sage advisers throughout history have offered their keys to success through books and newsletters. Some of these were academics like Benjamin Graham, who in his *Security Analysis* (written with David Dodd) first offered stock market wisdom in 1939; the book is now in its sixth edition. *The Intelligent Investor* followed in 1949. In both books, Graham offered tools for the analysis and valuation of securities, which were claims upon a business enterprise. Common stock represents an ownership claim on a portion of the business. Buyers share with other shareholders in the firm's profits or losses. Graham's writings, and others that followed, sought to explain the basis of value of a common share. But stock prices reflect a demand or supply based on what will be, not on what is at present.

What will be is not so easy to forecast. If an investor seeks a return via a gain in value, this requires information not usually available in the daily newspaper or television broadcast. If the investor seeks a return by receiving cash dividends distributed by the company, what will be the future dividends? Gaining returns through dividends or company growth in value requires research that may not be available in the usual media. Hence the rise of the stock-pick experts, whose reputation and media success often depend on past performance. This may also be their personal success or even no success.

Despite advice from experts, an entire market can be valued differently from one year or one time to the next. At one point in time, the outlook for corporate earnings can be very bright, and at another time, the outlook can be dismal. Did a new employment outlook indicate greater hiring by businesses, or did a decline in new jobs indicate an expected poor performance? What about changes in housing starts? Can changes in interest rates or an action by our central bank, the Federal Reserve, influence corporate earnings? Will a terrorist attack reduce values?

Regardless of the above difficulties facing common stock investors, the mind may look at the investment decision through rose-colored glasses—or, alternatively, through a depressed outlook on the market. It is the mind that must make a decision to buy or sell, delay or stay away. One mind will interpret information differently from another. It's like feeding the same information into different mind environments and usually coming to different decisions. A single mind environment changes over time, so a decision on investing may use new information differently at different times.

One week, an individual mind may see an interest-rate change announcement as a negative factor for an individual company or a sector of the economy or for stocks as a whole. The next week, this same investor might view it as a nonfactor in his decision. The same information is absorbed differently by different people and likely absorbed differently by the same investor at different times.

Personal emotions are part of that mind environment. Did he get out of the wrong side of the bed this morning? Did she feel guilty about excessive shopping the day before? Did the house cat pee on the kitchen floor? Is it a sunny day? Emotions are a part of the mind that influence buying and selling decisions.

Another influence on the investment decision—another part of the mind environment—may be input from friends who boast of their investment success. Much less common are their admissions of investment failures. The ego of the mind presents an information bias that usually declines to admit any sort of failure.

Aside from the above-mentioned inputs that influence an investment decision, individuals have a bias in the mind by which successful recent investments favor additional investment, while failure produces a bias against further investing. The investment decision is also heavily influenced by economic data inputs. Information about inflation expectations, unemployment, minimum wage, interest rates, and currencies impacts values or value beliefs. Also, values are influenced by the actions of federal and state governments.

Although our discussion here concentrates on the stock market, the mind also enters into all investment decisions—preferred stock, bonds, real estate, gold, land, antiques, and so forth. The mind will interact with an infinite variety of situations in which humans make investment decisions. If we were looking at bonds issued by states, cities, counties, and towns—called *municipal bonds*—the mind would look not only at different information at different times, but also personal emotions might weigh differently with different people. Emotions may play less of a role on the municipal bond investment decision than the common stock selection. But here we choose to emphasize in our discussion of the stock market that investment decisions are often heavily influenced by the mind.

Investors are also influenced by herd or mob behavior as well as by the investment media. If stock prices are rising, this usually results in a positive or optimistic outlook for the near future. But prices can go too far, creating a bubble or overbought condition or the reverse.

Market conditions have changed since the 1950s. No longer is the market dominated by the outlook of the collective mind of individual investors. Today, hedge funds, insurance companies, investment companies' mutual funds and closed-end funds, managed 401(k)s, and other institutions are the prime movers of the stock market. Nevertheless, Joe and Mary keep coming back to the stock market for investment returns, despite the risk. Stock market returns as a whole have averaged about 10 percent over recorded history.

This guide is meant to expose individual investors to the stock market and other investment alternatives as a primer. At no time during the reading of this book should the reader take any statement as a specific personal recommendation. This is not a complete course, only an overview. It is not a substitute for intensive study of the many aspects of the subject matter.

$ $

CHAPTER 2

$ $

Investment

For the individual who either saves or who comes into money, the question arises as to what to do with the funds if one does not wish to spend them now. Usually there exists enough demand for lending money that a saver can expect to be paid for postponing spending/consumption. The saver who withholds current consumption wants to be paid for giving up spending until the future.

Demand for money meets the supply of money in a marketplace, usually through some financial institution. The price in the market is the saver's rate of return on investment—an interest rate or yield to the investor. The market facilitates this by bringing a loan borrower and a saver together for a fee. It might be a borrower's mortgage that provides an additional security for the financial institution and its savings depositors. The rate paid by the borrower is the interest rate, which is the yield to the lender/supplier of funds. The suppliers usually are financial institutions who collect funds from savers and invests them. They are intermediaries between borrowers and savers. A bank, for example, needs to earn a return sufficient to pay its operating costs plus the payments to savers. It lives on the spread between the lending rate and the saving rate.

But there exist many investment alternatives beyond investing in mortgage loans directly or through a financial institution. Auto purchases often provide a need for funding and are an investment to a saver. Certificates of deposit from financial institutions, US Treasury bonds, and corporate preferred shares offer other investment opportunities.

Municipal bonds, as bonds of other governments like cities and school districts, also can be attractive investments. Bonds of corporations, pledges of small businesses, partial ownership in private or publicly owned companies (common stock/shares) also are alternatives. Investments vary in both uncertainty and returns.

Bonds are promises to pay by the borrower. The promises represent a legal responsibility. Failure to pay as promised is a default, and the justice system may take over the resolution of the parties involved. In corporate default, the issuer of the bonds faces not only possible liquidation (a dissolution) but also at least a reorganization of financial claims. Additionally, it can expect a poor credit rating, raising the cost of borrowing in any future financing. In a company/corporate reorganization, owners can be penalized or even removed from ownership. If bonds provided for specific assets pledged as their security, those assets may improve the prospects of a better settlement for the bondholders.

An investment implies a commitment by the investor, perhaps for a defined period of time. Risk and uncertainty, however, vary widely.

A very important aspect of investment is that the returns are often paid on a regular basis—daily, monthly, quarterly, semiannually, or annually, for example. As a result, investors may have the opportunity for their return to grow at an increasing rate. If they are able to reinvest the return received each period in the same asset, the amount invested will grow more quickly. Even in a savings account, returns can be reinvested and thus increase in value over time.

Assume $100.00 is invested at 4 percent to become $104.00 at the end of year one, and then reinvested; $104.00(1.04) = $108.16 is the value at year two and a $219.11 can be payment at the end of twenty years. That's an extra $39.11 above the simple $80.00 return in twenty years. This is called *compounding*, where periodic payments are reinvested each period. Not reinvesting would provide just the $4.00 times twenty years or $80.00 return on the original $100.00 invested. By spending the return each year instead of reinvesting, you lose the benefit of compounding for additional returns. If you are saving for retirement, start young and let your money grow by reinvesting the periodic returns.

In contrast to investment, the term *speculation* implies a greater uncertainty in seeking a larger return. But one type of speculation can play a very useful role in the financial world. The speculator contributes to the stabilization of asset prices by correcting incorrectly priced common stock rights and stock options based on underlying stock values, as well as contributing to commodity seasonal price stability.

For example, consider corn prices. The corn crop is usually harvested in the late summer months. Much of it is harvested at about the same time every year, depressing market prices at that time. Left alone, the prices for corn in August/September would be very low, and in January, prices would be very high. But speculators buy when they believe the supply is high and prices are low, store it, and sell when they think the supply is low and prices are higher. This results in balancing out the supply throughout the year and reducing seasonal price fluctuations.

Gambling, in contrast to speculating, is a commitment, usually for a very short period. The alternative outcomes can often be very clear. Before the horserace, the odds are published. A toss of the dice at a casino provides the odds of any result. Still, gamblers may enjoy the risk of outcomes; they find entertainment value. This is much different from investors who try to balance return and risk to suit themselves. The host who offers the gambling event opportunity usually takes a percentage of the amount wagered. Unless you have some superior knowledge, over the long run, you must lose the gamble, because the host makes money by taking a portion of the risky results.

$ $

CHAPTER 3

$ $

Profit

The word *profit* may be considered a dirty word by some. Profit, like other returns—such as interest, dividends, and yield—is a payment for giving up consumption, for saving, and for bearing uncertainty or risk. In any business, before we can label an amount profit, we should make sure all costs are subtracted from revenues.

Just as a bank receives payment for the lending of funds to borrowers, there is no profit for a bank unless it covers all its costs. In this bank example, the costs include payment to depositors for not consuming. But bank costs also include such costs as accounting, recording, salaries, the building, and the use of equipment. In addition, there is the cost of the bank owners' capital. The owners who put up the money to establish the bank expect a return like any other investment. However, accounting does not include this as a cost in measuring business income.

Return on an investment should always include a return for giving up consumption. This pure return can be considered free of risk. But the return may also include payment for bearing various types of risk. *Credit risk* is the risk or uncertainty of repayment of the nominal dollar amount invested.

For a bank, the deposits are an IOU—a promise to pay by the bank. Although the deposits are insured by the federally created Federal Deposit Insurance Corporation (FDIC) and the equivalent for credit unions, there is a concern that this insurance could fail. There are limits to the amount this FDIC insurance can pay. Thus, savers who place their money with the financial institution have some risk of loss of their deposit. Given that FDIC insurance provides some worth, these deposits have low credit risk. If the FDIC could not meet all claims—as in the case of a national bank disaster—losses would occur .In addition to receiving a pure rate of interest, savers as investors will also need to be paid for credit risk—a small amount for most financial institutions. But not all investments have such low credit risk.

For some investments, the returns are a fixed rate of interest on the principal amount. Once the investment is purchased, the rate of interest to maturity is fixed. Your are stuck with that return. Afterwards if the market rate of interest for that risk and maturity may change. If the market rate is higher, then your rate of return is worth less. Fixed rate of investments are subject to that *interest rate risk.*

The owners of the bank who put up the money for the bank have no such direct insurance. They incur losses if costs exceed revenue, and therefore their investment in the bank has a larger credit risk than depositors. Owners who start a small or even a good-sized business face yet a higher credit risk.

Given that savers who deposit their savings in a bank need small compensation for credit risk, they do have another risk as they withdraw their dollars. The risk is that the price of goods and services they consume have risen in during the time the bank held their deposits. Where prices are expected to rise, depositors want to be compensated for these inflation expectations—or more specifically, the risk of inflation. Therefore, in addition to credit risk, savers want to be paid for *inflation risk*, also called *purchasing power risk.*

For most investment alternatives available to savers, there exist markets where suppliers and demanders of funds meet. For example, there is a real estate market, a market for antiques, a market for municipal bonds, and a market for common stock. Sometimes these markets have large price changes not warranted by the fundamental changes in credit or inflation risk. Human emotions can enter the marketplace, causing excessive variations in price, whether declines or advances. This threat is called *market risk.*

Finally, there may be a risk in liquidation. For some investments, the purchase may involve some uncertainty about the ability to sell the asset/investment efficiently—that is, quickly and at a fair price. With bank deposits, one can usually count on a quick, easy withdrawal. For a 1920 Bentwood rocker, on the other hand, a sale could be difficult; even if possible, it would likely take some time. This we can call *liquidation risk*. With the arrival of eBay and the Internet, many more investments can find a reasonable market. But if I buy the antique rocker as an investment, I would want a little more return to allow for the risk of selling my investment.

So what is profit, if we give up current consumption for the pure rate of interest and invest in an asset that involves credit risk, inflation risk, market risk and liquidation risk?

If we invest in an asset in another country, we expect some return for assuming the risk of a change in the currency exchange rate upon liquidation—thus *currency risk*. For many investments, the risks can be quite low, as is true with many financial assets, including some stocks, bonds, and deposits in financial institutions.

Studies have estimated the pure rate of interest (no risk) to average about 2 percent. Given the central bank's objective inflation rate of 2 percent, and 0 percent for domestic currency risk, we can add to the 4 percent the return for credit, market, and liquidation risk which varies with the investment.

Not everyone measures profit the same. Accounting rules provide their definition as to what is profit for a business. Economists look to state it differently, as profit is after all costs, including the cost of the owner's equity investment. To governmental taxing authorities, returns may be taxable, whether they are called profit or not.

PART ONE

Publicly Held Common Stock as an Investment

$ $

CHAPTER 4

$ $

The Stock Market

Common stock represents a part-ownership in a business. Stock (shares) in corporations are usually bought and sold in various stock markets. The New York Stock Exchange (NYSE) provides a market for the shares of many larger companies, both domestic and foreign. To enter this market as a buyer or seller of part of a business, by buying already issued and publicly available common stock, you need to contact a member of the stock exchange where it is traded—that is, bought and sold. That person or firm can act as an agent for you to buy or sell the shares.

These agents (stockbrokers) are salespersons in a merchandizing business. Like any other retailer, they earn their living through sales, usually by collecting a fee/commission for the service they provide. Understand that their income depends on sales to you and others or purchases from you and others. They provide a service to the investor by buying or selling these shares as directed. You may also ask them for help in locating the kind of business you want to become a part-owner in, and you may want them to explain their view of the pros and cons of a particular business or industry. It is a retail financial store, buying and selling for a fee. But the decision is yours, not theirs.

One aspect of owning shares in a corporation is that the liquidation or sale of the investment is usually quick and efficient. That means the investment is liquid. This quality of service can vary. The emphasis is on the word *usually*.

If you need help in selecting a business to participate in as a shareholder, aside from the salesperson/broker, you can seek out investment advisers who offer recommendations. There are many who make a living by selling a newsletter of advice. They recommend businesses that they may believe are worth more than the market says—or at least worth the price. Again, the emphasis here is on selling their advice. It's another merchandizing institution.

Although market price itself, much of the time, is a good indicator of value, analysts/advisers believe the investments they recommend are fully valued or undervalued for reasons they advance. You don't need to rely on finding undervalued business. Selecting a properly valued business that fits your desire for growth and/or income can be your goal. Analysts/advisers can provide ideas and opinions on undervalued or overvalued alternatives. We will look more at advisers later in this book. Always remember that the investment choice is yours, not the adviser's, unless you have delegated decisions to them.

The NYSE is the largest and best-known trading venue. Although exchanges exist in many countries where shares are traded, many of the largest and most recognized company shares in the world are traded on the NYSE. Only members can trade there. But for a fee, the exchange member or member firm accepts your trade requests.

The second-largest trading market is the NASDAQ, which is not a place but an electronic market. For shares to be traded in the NASDAQ, a company must be registered with US Securities and Exchange Commission. It must also have at least three market-makers—firms (brokers and dealers) that stand ready to buy and sell the stock. In addition, the company must meet the minimum requirements for assets, capital, publicly held shares, and number of shareholders. NASDAQ also computes an index (NASDAQ Composite) to trace the movement of shares as a whole listed in the NASDAQ.

Other much-watched indices of share prices include the Standard & Poor's 500 and the Dow Jones Industrials, an average of the share prices of thirty large companies.

Investors in publicly owned companies are not immune from emotion. They can be guilty of being overly optimistic or pessimistic about a business or the entire market for shares of businesses. Hence, prices of business-share ownership can occasionally be overinflated or undervalued, a boom or bust, because of entire market excesses. Such volatility moves returns and values up and down, but the very long-run average return on publicly held common stock in the United States tends to average about 10 percent per year. The emphasis should be on long-run and average.

CHAPTER 5

$ $

Investing in Common Stock

Although the long-run average return on common stock investment is about 10 percent, that does not mean that everyone who buys common stock can expect a 10 percent return. If you rely on your luck or instincts, you should expect a result much different from the average. The return you achieve can also vary depending how long a period you are invested. If you take a very cautious, conservative approach, your return will likely be less than the average, for assuming less risk than the overall average. And the return can vary depending on the date that you choose to terminate your ownership.

There are no promises. Uncertainty usually exists. You must be able accept days when the value of your portfolio of stocks fluctuates.

Investors usually choose a group of shares, called a *portfolio*, according to their investment objectives. Investors who are young and early in their working lives, can rely on long periods of investment before being called upon to cash in. Those near or at retirement age generally choose a less volatile portfolio, that will be less affected by the end date or the date when they begin to use the funds.

The price of a share of common stock is heavily influenced by the expected earnings of the company. Earnings are measured by generally accepted accounting principles (GAAP). Financial reporting is usually presented using GAAP and may be presented for trailing period of twelve months (TTM)—that is, the most recent twelve months. The total earnings or income is typically divided by the number of shares of common stock outstanding to provide the earnings per share (EPS).

Even using GAAP, companies have some latitude in how they measure earnings. The price of the stock divided by the EPS is the price-earnings ratio (P/E). This P/E indicates how many years of those earnings equals price. P/E is a measure of how expensive the market values a share to be. P/E ratios, for a market average, measure 14 and up—depending, in part, on how optimistic the investing public is at the time about future earnings.

If the P/E of Plodding Company is 6, then we ask, why is it so cheap, or is it undervalued by the market? Is it going broke? If the P/E of Delightful Company is 28, why is it so expensive? Is its future for increased earnings so bright?

A publicly held company often forecasts its next year's earnings—its EPS. If it earns less than the forecast, the stock price will usually decline, assuming the price of the stock had already valued the company's forecast. Earnings surprises usually result in changes in share prices.

Some corporations issue preferred stock. Preferred stocks are a promise to pay specific dividends and a promise to pay before any dividends will be paid to the common stockholders. A 5 percent stock pays 5 percent of the par/stated price of the stock, before it can consider paying a dividend to common shareholders.

CHAPTER 6

Buying and Selling

The stock market is where agents of buyers and sellers of shares meet. In today's electronic world, it need not be a physical place. But it is often viewed as a place. The New York Stock Exchange is a place where buyers and sellers, through their agents, meet to buy and sell thousands of different stocks. Other corporations' shares trade elsewhere. The NASDAQ is an electronic exchange.

A trade means a buyer and seller have agreed on an exchange of money for shares, or shares for money, of common stock in a corporation. A *bid* is what the buyer is willing to pay, and an *ask* is the offer price of a prospective seller.

Suppose Alice says that if I will vacuum her messy car, she will make and give me a cherry pie. We agree to the transaction. It is a trade, and we both think it is a good trade. We both believe we each gain.

Now consider two countries, Able and Baker. Able has a great climate and soil for producing apples but has no oil. Baker has oil and lousy conditions for growing apples. The consumers in both countries want to trade apples for oil and oil for apples. With a trade, Able's consumers have both apples and oil and are happier than when they had apples alone and no oil. Baker's consumers are happier having apples and oil rather than oil alone. Trade is a win–win transaction for both parties.

Even if Able has some oil but it is difficult and costly to extract, and/or Baker can grow apples but not good ones, trade will take place. If Baker can easily get oil out of the ground and Able can grow great apples, trade is a win for the consumers of both countries.

Of course, the advantages of the exchange of apples and oil must be sufficient to overcome the transportation costs for trade to take place. Governments of both countries could interfere by placing barriers to trade, causing losses to consumers. Tariffs, taxes on imports, or other restrictions only reduce the wins for consumers.

This win–win trade also takes place in the stock market. One party to a trade wants to buy into ownership of a particular corporation, and one party wants to sell an ownership. Such win–win trades also takes place within a country and between countries. The buyer buys shares that have already been issued by the corporation from an investor-owner who wishes to sell.

In the United States, oranges do not grow in the state of Washington, but the state does produce apples, airplanes, and computer software. There is trade between Washington, the apple producer, and Florida where oranges are grown as long as the costs of transportation are not excessive enough to stop the movement of goods between regions and states. The United States is a free-trade zone, allowing goods to move freely from one region to another. There are no government barriers to trade in legal goods and services. Such trades or exchanges are a gain for consumers in Washington who enjoy oranges and a benefit for consumers in Florida who like the availability of apples. Sales tax differences can reduce trade. Trade, a purchase, a sale, a transaction, is a win for both parties.

One of the great economic advantages of a large country like the United States is the existence of a large free market. If one builds a better mousetrap, there will be a huge market available in which to sell your product. This is one of the incentives to invent and create. Mousetraps are sold for money, and money is used to buy other goods and services or saved to spend later.

The trade/transaction benefit also exists for individual consumers. If consumers buy shoes at a retail store for $50, that means they are willing to part with at least $50 in exchange for the shoes. If the store offers them at $50, it must be willing to part with them at that price. The sale contributes to the store's revenue and hopefully profits. This exchange or transaction is a win for the consumer and a win for the store. In fact, all transactions, by definition, are wins for both buyers and sellers.

Even if there is a sales tax or a value-added tax imposed by a government, the parties of the exchange will pay it if they still agree to the exchange. But what about a government property tax or an income tax on money? Is that exchange (money for what?), a gain for both? At first thought, it may be a win for the taxing government but not for the payer. Does an individual consumer gain by paying money to the government? Are the benefits of justice, defense, infrastructure, and so on, enough to make it a win for a citizen to give up money to the government as a tax? For the individual paying the tax, it also can be a win to avoid the IRS or unwanted legal action. So the tax exchange must also be a good win for both the payer and the government. A trade of common stock, any purchase and sale, a swap, an exchange, or a transaction benefits both parties.

$ $
# CHAPTER 7
$ $
Cash Is King

Generally accepted accounting principles (GAAP) guide companies large and small, in reporting earnings/income and earnings per share. This income and future expectations of income are used by investors to value a business. Yet the accounting discretion allowed in inventory valuation, depreciation, depletion, and intangible assets permits some accounting management of reported income. Such management can cloud investor valuation. If the company chooses to select accounting methods that favor their appearance, stock price may benefit. But often good analysts can see through the subterfuge.

Some accounting adjustments made to earnings result in misleading information on true profitability. Earnings before interest and taxes (EBIT) figures may solve some of the confusion about the profitability of the company, but cash flow may be even better.

Another measure of a company's success is cash flow—the net of all cash payments. Cash is a fact not subject to different accounting measurements. Cash flow cannot lie. It must be available to meet interest payments and other cash demands of the company.

Some analysts use cash flow as a preferred measure of profitability over net income. Both are usually provided by analysts on a per-share basis. Cash measures the ability of the company to meet cash demands and the ability to provide returns to its owners (shareholders) as dividends.

Both interest and dividends, as returns to capital, usually require cash payment. If a company pays a dividend in shares of the company instead of a cash dividend, the number of shares increase and the company retains cash. If the company pays cash dividends, there is no uncertainty about the amount of cash to be provided.

If an investor relies only on earnings, the numbers could be a less-certain guide because of management of accounting practices. It's not that GAAP are faulty; the accounting profession must have rules that need to be applied to many different businesses and circumstances. GAAP, therefore, allow some latitude in the treatment of different events.

Some common stock investors choose to select only cash-paying companies—the cash-dividend payers. They heavily favor those companies with a long record of steady or growing cash-dividend payments. Payment of cash provides confidence in return on investment. Cash flow reflects the ability of the company to pay cash returns to investors, whereas reliance entirely upon reported earnings may leave some degree of uncertainty about a company's cash-paying desire and ability.

$ $

CHAPTER 8

$ $

Agents, Brokers, and Dealers

A *broker-dealer* is a person or firm in the business of buying and selling securities. You can hire a broker to access the appropriate market for you to execute your purchase or sale of securities. Acting as an agent, the broker charges a fee for that service, so you would have to pay the purchase price plus the fee or, if selling, you get the sale price less the fee. An agent legally acts on behalf of the client. The fees are set by the broker firm for all clients.

Usually, transactions in securities listed on an exchange like the New York Stock Exchange are agency transactions. The execution of the purchase or sale of a security listed on the exchange are regularly done only by a member of the exchange. If your broker-dealer in not a member, they will use another broker who is a member to execute the purchase or sale.

There are full-service broker firms and discount broker firms. A full-service broker charges a higher fee than a discount broker. The discount broker may provide some services to help you but expects that you can make your own decisions with whatever information is available without much help or advice. The full-service broker may undertake research on your behalf and can even manage your account if you grant that authority, without your approving each individual transaction decision.

With your permission, a broker managing the account—even retirement accounts like IRAs and 401(k)s—can buy or sell securities for the account as long as the investments are suitable for your investment goals. In this case, the broker has some incentive to make numerous transactions on your behalf, as the account manager generates fees on each transaction. As of April 2017, unless revoked, brokers managing retirement accounts must meet a higher standard for making managed transactions for these accounts. The broker acting after that date must manage the account as a fiduciary. The transactions must therefore be in the best interest of the client, not just suitable.

This is an important distinction, but these new rules apply only to retirement accounts. For others, be on your guard. The new rules involve more details that the investor should evaluate before setting up a managed retirement account.

Most brokers also act as dealers and are referred to as broker-dealers. Broker-dealers may also undertake the role of investment bankers—raising money for businesses. They usually have ready access to investors as clients. The initial public offering is one example of this role.

Dealers buy and sells selected securities from their inventory like a retail store. The dealer acts as a principal, selling to you or buying from you. The dealer is not an agent. The dealer's sale price is not tied to the dealer's cost. Demand and supply, as well as the competition, will determine the bid and offering prices.

The same person can be an agent on some transactions and a dealer for other transactions. A dealer should be distinguished from a trader. A dealer makes a business of buying and selling a particular security at its stated prices from its inventory. A trader seeks to gain from changes in the price.

The dealer market is where multiple dealers post their bid and ask prices; hence, it is a competitive market. The dealer market consists of two levels. There is an interdealer market where the spread between bid and ask is narrower than the retail market. Securities not listed on an exchange trade in the dealer market and vary considerably in market quality. Those not often traded usually have a wider spread between bid and ask. They are less competitive, and therefore the liquidity risk can become important.

All brokers, dealers, broker-dealers, and other individuals and firms participating in the business must be registered with the US Securities and Exchange Commission. They are held to provide prompt execution of orders, disclose conflicts of interest, disclose pertinent information, and charge fees and prices that are reasonable given market conditions. These individuals or salesmen in a firm may also be called *representatives* or *account executives*. They must be licensed and pass examinations reflecting a basic knowledge of the securities business. This is in no way a guarantee of the success of their clients.

CHAPTER 9

Investment Information

Investors need investment information to make investment decisions. Ideally it would be easily available, as current as possible and unbiased. Therefore, we need to find reporting sources. In today's Internet world, publicly held companies have websites you can access. As public companies, they are required by the US Securities and Exchange Commission to file a 10Q report every quarter. It discloses the company's revenue, expenses, and profit, as well as other details. The data reported is generated according to generally accepted accounting principles.

The quarterly report represents one-fourth of the calendar year and is often released after March, June, September, and December. A minority of companies report on a fiscal year, not calendar, because of the seasonality of their operations. Obviously, shareholders and prospective shareholders would like to see increases in revenue and profit compared to the previous quarter and the same quarter a year ago, as some companies have a seasonal change in operations. Of all the data, the shareholders, as owners, have a major interest in profits, also called *income* or *earnings*. And better yet, their interest is in the profits/earnings per share. This EPS is calculated as total earnings divided by the number of shares outstanding.

Your investing agent, such as your bank or broker, will usually have this information for you, covering many periods and perhaps charts of performance and other information.

At your local library, you may find investment information in the reference area. The library may subscribe to investment services like

Value Line Investment Survey and *Morningstar*. In addition to rating stocks and funds on risk and performance, these publications may provide commentary on the economy, major sectors of the market, and/or industries. If your interest is in insurance companies, the *A. M. Best* periodical can be helpful.

If you are interested in bonds, investment services like *Moody's, Standard & Poor's, and Fitch* evaluate and rate corporate and governments bonds, including municipal bonds. Also, several investment periodicals provide articles on many aspects of investing. Some of these established periodicals are *Barron's, Wall Street Journal, Investors Business Daily*, and *Forbes*. Their interest is in subscriptions, and they apparently have no sector, industry, or company ties to bias their reporting.

$ $

CHAPTER 10

$ $

Diversification

The old saying "Don't put all your eggs in one basket" is meant to promote *diversification*. In the investment world, it means put your money in more than one, or even many, investments. Diversification can reduce the volatility of the value of the basket/portfolio without surrendering return. But often, you give up some average return to reduce ups and downs.

For the investment in common stock, there are many alternatives that allow you to reduce volatility and increase relative (not total) stability in the value of your portfolio of shares. It's like choosing an air conditioning business as well as a heating business—putting them together reduces the seasonal ups and downs. Technically, for shares, it's a matter of building a portfolio of uncorrelated businesses. Selecting a blanket-selling business along with a coat-selling business is not a good choice with respect to seasonal fluctuations; their sales would likely go up and down together. Their sales are said to be correlated during the season.

Not only can you diversify among shares of different companies in different industries, you can further diversify by selecting unrelated investment alternatives to further insulate your investment portfolio from fluctuating prices. You could add corporate bonds, US Treasury bonds and notes, municipal bonds, preferred stock, mortgages, certificates of deposit, and so on. This would further decrease the volatility of an entire bundle of assets. However, in doing so, you should expect some change in the returns of the whole portfolio, as each class of investment has a different credit risk, interest rate risk, and the like.

Diversification is sometimes achieved by a prescribed asset allocation of investments in common stocks, foreign currencies, real estate, farmland, coins, antiques, art, gold, and other commodities. More on this later. If you choose to diversify, you may surrender some expected returns. But a few investors choose to concentrate their investments and not diversify.

Investors who are confident of large returns on a single investment may choose to put all their eggs in one basket and monitor that basket very closely. These aggressive investors may even go to the extreme of borrowing to add to their investment in the asset, increasing the uncertainty of final returns. Such leveraging is not conservative. It can end in financial disaster if the prediction fails.

Concentration could be profitable, however, if you were sure of your results. Unfortunately, these so-called sure things are rare. Much of your investment life finds you waiting for that big opportunity. Most of those who have gone this investing route say that only a few times in life do such opportunities arise—and if they do, often a great deal of patience and sticking to your beliefs is required.

$ $

CHAPTER 11

$ $

Diversification in Bundles

Although the New York Stock Exchange is the world's largest and most famous market, many more less-well-known markets exist. It is well worth your while to know about these markets and the value they can offer to investors. The exchanges may list corporate bonds for trading as well as stock options, closed-end investment companies, exchange-traded notes, and exchange-traded funds (ETFs). Much of the trading is done electronically without a person involved.

An *ETF*, Exchange Traded Fund, is a specific portfolio. Such funds allow an investor to, in effect, own a bundle of stocks in a specific industry, a specific sector/region, a specific country, or with a special investment goal. For example, if you wish to own some common stock of companies in India but do not want to rely on selecting an individual company or companies, you could buy an ETF whose stock exchange trade symbol is IFN. You could make your own portfolio with a single ETF or combination of ETFs. If you wanted to buy into the biotech industry, you could select an ETF whose trade symbol is PBE, and you do not have to select one particular company.

You can select a commodity ETF, a currency ETF, a fixed-income ETF, or a real estate ETF. You can select an ETF that tracks an equity index, like the Standard & Poor's 500 index of equities. An ETF provides opportunities for diversification with just a single transaction.

An *investment company* is either a closed-end fund, where the number of shares are fixed, or an open-end fund (referred to as a mutual fund), where the number of shares changes as buyers and sellers enter or depart as owners. Investment companies also offer opportunities for diversification.

A *closed-end fund* is managed to achieve a specified investment goal. With a fixed number of outstanding shares, the fund can be traded on an exchange, just as an ETF or individual company like Coca Cola would be. The value of the investment company shares can be calculated as the sum of the market value of the securities and other assets it holds divided by the number of shares outstanding, called *net asset value (NAV) per share*.

NAV per share may not always equal the exchange-traded price of the fund. The market price of the closed-end fund often is less than its NAV, offering a discount to its value. As long as it pays out at least 90 percent of its investment income, the investment company is not taxed by the IRS, the US Internal Revenue Service. It is also required to pay out at least 98 percent of its realized capital gains in order to avoid company taxation. This pass-through of income to the shareholder assures taxation at the investor level.

A *mutual fund*—an open-end investment company, most often—sells its shares at NAV plus, perhaps, a sales markup or load, and buys back its shares at NAV. This type of investment company is buying and selling its own shares, and therefore the number of shares outstanding changes from day to day. There exist some no-load companies, although all have some sort of management fee that is taken from the fund. Many of these shares can be traded through an exchange or other markets. Investors may select a mutual fund whose goal or investment objective suits their risk and income objective.

Most libraries subscribe to an investment service that provides information about alternative funds—their goals, risks, and success. You can also use the Internet for research. Usually an investor seeks a comparative analysis of several funds, which a library resource may be able to present, saving you some time. These funds provide diversification without the investor having to buy a bundle of individual securities. Buying and selling such a fund reduces the transaction cost over what one would pay making one's own bundle of shares of individual companies.

As with each of these diversification funds, ETFs, and investment companies (closed and open/mutual funds), the management of the portfolio is necessary to meet the investment goals. The more active the management, the more the annual expense charged to the fund, reducing income. In comparing funds, make sure you have included in your analysis all the fees that may be involved. Again, you can find expense ratios of funds at your library or usually on the Internet. Do not ignore these expense ratios and possible other fees in the selection of your investment company.

$ $

CHAPTER 12

$ $

Portfolio Management

A portfolio, in a financial view, is a collection of financial assets. In the common, more narrow sense, it is a portfolio of common stocks. An additional topic of discussion is a portfolio of all financial assets, which will be discussed in chapter 42 on allocation. It is sometimes referred to as *asset allocation*. Or one could call them the *stock portfolio* and the *full asset/financial portfolio*.

A common stock traded in a market can be expected to change in price as the market as a whole changes in price. One measure of market prices is the Standard & Poor's 500 (S&P 500), a stock index of five hundred share prices. When this index rises or falls, it is interpreted as the market price of stocks changing, or, as they say, the market is rising or falling. A bull market means that stock prices are trending upward; a bear market means stock prices are trending downward. There are other indicators of market prices, the Dow (Dow Jones Industrial Average) being one. An important point here is that the movement of market prices as a whole, usually contributes something to every stock price's movement, although it contributes more to some stock prices than others.

Some stock prices are more sensitive to market changes than others. If you are looking for this attribute in a stock, some financial media sources will provide a measure of market sensitivity called *beta*. A stock with a beta of one(1), can be expected to fluctuate about the same percentage amount as the market as a whole, as reflected in the S&P 500. A higher beta value means the stock price is very sensitive and should accentuate the market's moves. With a beta of less than one, you should expect the stock price to fluctuate less than the market as a whole.

But stock prices also move independent of market-induced price changes. They have non-market-induced price fluctuations. As a portfolio manager, you should be aware that each stock will have its own moves, as investors and traders push a stock price one way or the other. One good thing about these unique price fluctuations is that they move differently; price moves are not correlated to each other to some degree.

If you were to select stocks in the same industry that compete with each other, it is likely their stock prices would move somewhat together. That is, they would be highly correlated. If you were to select stocks in different industries, you might expect that they would each move quite independently except for the entire market's influence. They would be low-correlated with each other. Your portfolio would be more diversified. There is that word again: diversification! You diversify your portfolio by selecting more than a single stock and stocks in businesses unrelated to each other.

Many financial advisers recommend putting only 4 to 5 percent of your stock portfolio in any one stock. This would mean holding twenty to twenty-five different company common shares. For many investors, this is not realistic. How are you going to come up with that many excellent opportunities? If you were to force that on yourself, you would likely end up either holding a lot of idle cash waiting for many good opportunities or forcing immediate diversification into twenty to twenty-five stocks, resulting in an index of the stock market and average returns. The portfolio beta should converge on the value of one for the entire portfolio. This large number of different shares reflects the limit of your ability to watch no more than twenty to twenty-five.

My studies have found that, on average, you can eliminate about 90 percent of this nonmarket volatility by choosing only ten randomly selected stocks. If you can stay away from doubling up in one industry, you should consider your portfolio diversified with around ten different businesses. You may want to hold enough idle liquid funds that you can take advantage of opportunities as they arise. But if you are fully invested in about ten stocks, a new opportunity will require selling enough to make room for the one you cannot pass up.

A difficulty with stock portfolio management is avoiding over-concentration in a few industries. Opportunities often come in one or a few industries at a time. If this happens, you face the choice of either taking on more risk or expanding the number of holdings toward the higher number of twenty to twenty-five to more easily achieve satisfactory diversification.

The full asset/financial portfolio, or asset allocation, includes all assets representing the financial wealth of the investor. Such a portfolio may include cash (and equivalent), a common stock portfolio, preferred stocks, corporate bonds, government and municipal bonds, real estate, precious metals, and so on. In effect, this division of investor assets is a more extensive degree of diversification, as these asset classes do not move together in value changes.

$ $

CHAPTER 13

$ $

Initial Public Offering

Companies' shares are usually not born ready for trading. Typically, a business begins by forming a corporation whose shares are held by the principals involved in creating the business. The corporation is only a privately held company at first. That is, shares are not held by the public. As the company grows, it may reach the size where it needs more capital.

Borrowing has its limits for a young company. The corporation will eventually need more ownership capital. Also, the principals of the firm may want public participation in ownership as confirmation of the value of their enterprise. They can offer the public a chance to express its view of value through the exchange of investor cash for share ownership. Occasionally, smaller private companies can sell their new shares themselves after government approval. But raising large amounts of new money calls for an *initial public offering* (IPO), using professional help.

The principals and officers of the company seeking an IPO will usually seek the aid of a financial specialist firm called an *investment banker*. The investment banker can help arrange a sale in conformance with the legal requirements for disclosure of information about the company selling its shares. An information document, called a *prospectus*, is prepared for approval by the regulatory authorities. The investment banker has the necessary contacts to find prospective investors.

Once the registration and prospectus are approved by the government body, the sale may take place to investors wishing to buy into ownership of the company. It is important that the investment banker seek a wide distribution of shares to many investors to provide a good aftermarket. The banker does not want the shares sold to a few large investors who might threaten the management or the original creators of the company, or limit active trading.

The investment banker will offer advice to the company on the asking price for the shares to be sold. On the one hand, the company selling its shares wants a price that does not let new investors share ownership too cheaply. It also wants enough new funds to help the company continue its growth. But the investment banker will want to make sure the price is attractive enough to encourage sufficient investors for a rapid, successful sale of all the shares proposed. The investment banker will want assurance that the sale can be completed the same day as the offering and may guarantee the company the complete sale of all the shares planned, another factor influencing the selling price.

A successful IPO will assure that shares are sold to many investors, scattered widely. The investment banker and the company will seek to distribute the shares to a large number of independent investors. This broad distribution should support an active aftermarket trading behavior. The original principals now can visualize a public recognition and valuation of their enterprise. A good public market adds potential liquidity to the common stock holdings of its investors.

The stock sold in the IPO may initially be traded not on an exchange, but in what is called the *over-the-counter market*. The investment banker or bankers involved with the IPO will most likely respond to any buyers and sellers interested in aftermarket transactions. They will become market makers, offering to buy or sell the stock.

Stock exchanges may offer a higher-quality market for stocks. They will list the stock for trading if the company's application for listing is approved. For example, the requirements for NASDAQ listing are a minimum of three market makers who stand by to buy or sell the stock at its bid and ask price. The listing also requires a minimum asset size, a minimum capital size, a minimum number of publicly held shares, and a minimum number of stockholders. The requirements for listing on the New York Stock Exchange are higher; it tends to attract larger companies for trading.

For the offering of common stock, both the selling company and the investment banker set a price for the limited number of shares to be sold and the day they are available for sale. Those who are willing to pay the release price or more can expect to be allotted shares for purchase in the company. Those who refuse to pay that much will not receive shares. Should the demand be greater than the number of shares available at the release price, the aftermarket price will likely rise as investors who were not allotted shares to buy do so in the aftermarket.

Pricing in an IPO and the rationing of shares to be sold is an interesting event. If the share price in the aftermarket rises significantly, one might conclude a pricing error has been made. Was the company upset that new public shareholders paid too cheap a price? Perhaps. More likely, the excess demand for shares that increased the stock price in the aftermarket was caused by an emotional exuberance about the company's prospects, which may be followed by a disappointing later price.

In an example, Darling, Inc., a six-year-old company, had developed a love potion that produced a healthy growth in sales and positive earnings in its early life. Valuation based on its earnings and growth by its investment banker was $12 a share. But the investment banker's survey of demand based on the preliminary prospectus indicated a huge demand for the shares and an estimated aftermarket price of $17. Although the company could raise about 40 percent more money on the sale of shares at 17, the company agreed with the banker that the share price in the aftermarket would eventually fall to its more fundamental value, making these new investors very unhappy. If the aftermarket price fell from $17 to $12, it likely would subject the company to many shareholder complaints. So the company and the banker agreed to release the shares for sale at $12.

PART TWO

Investing and the Economy

$ $

CHAPTER 14

$ $

The Economy

The state of the economy influences earnings and companies being traded. In addition, the economy affects the participants in the market who may look on the future optimistically or pessimistically, as rosy or sad. So the stock market does not move just with changes in expected earnings. It can move with changes in earnings expectations and the emotion of the economy's participants—the buyers and sellers. The market as measured by the Standard and Poor's 500 often overshoots or undershoots what one would expect with changes in companies. Changes in personal incomes, exports, imports, government spending, strikes, taxation, and elections can bring about shifts in economic outlook, causing recession or inflation.

But the economy of a locality, a region, a nation, and even other nations in the world also influences stock market expectations. Wherever companies do business, the economy is going to impact success or failure. The total spending of consumers, businesses, and governments reflects the demand for goods and services. This demand impacts employment, the price of goods and services, and the price of the resources used to create them.

Money (currency) and credit facilitates this activity. The demand for goods and services can be influenced by the availability of money and credit. Hence, central banks, like the Federal Reserve in the United States, seek to influence the demand for goods and services by changing monetary conditions, including the availability of money and credit and the price of money and credit (interest rates).

But money, credit, and interest rates alone do not determine demand for goods and services. Demand is also impacted by rules and regulations; optimism and pessimism; demographics; technology; and even the weather. All factors are interconnected. A whim for smartphones in Timbuktu can have ripple effects throughout the world, not just on currency exchange rates but on labor employment in Japan and resource output in Australia. Economic forecasting is not only complex but virtually impossible to do with precision very far in the future.

The stock market may involve excessive declines, perhaps due to human extensions of conditions and/or emotions. This can provide opportunities to buy shares of companies on the cheap. But such buying when the market has declined excessively is difficult to execute free of pessimistic emotion. While some stock fortune-tellers claim to know when the stock market hits bottom, predicting the stock market is even tougher than predicting the economy.

Economic excesses can also be created by governments and its managed paper money. By 2015, the central bank in the United States had increased the money supply approximately 400 percent since 2006. The government doubled the national debt outstanding from 2007 to 2015. Labor participation in the workforce declined every year since 2007 to the lowest since the 1970s, even though the unemployment rate declined to below 5 percent of those looking for work. Over forty million were reported to be supported by government-issued food stamps.

The Federal Reserve, the central bank of the United States, has been charged by congressional legislation to monitor the economy and attempt to manage it with respect to unemployment and inflation. However, the mix of investor emotions, changing earnings of companies, and government attempts to change employment and price levels make stock-market forecasts in a national and world economy near worthless. If economists cannot predict the state of the economy, how can we expect psychologists to forecast the stock market? As individuals, we accept the fact that it fluctuates; it goes up and down.

$ $

CHAPTER 15

$ $

Price Rations

During World War II, households had coupons that were used to limit the purchase of things like sugar, shoes, coffee, gasoline, and meat. We could buy these items only if we had the government-issued coupons to make a purchase. It wasn't that we couldn't afford to buy more or did not want to buy more; we could only buy the coupon-limited amounts. Prices were thus determined by the government. This coupon-rationing limited the effective demand to the amount available, even if some wanted more at that price. Everyone was treated equally. The plan was that you could not buy more regardless of how much money you had.

When we think of rationing, we visualize distributing a valuable commodity that is insufficient to meet all buyers at a certain price. The demand is limited by government-issued coupons. A so-called "black market" could exist if some sales were made by illegal suppliers to those buyers who were willing to pay more and bypass the legal market.

But price of an item can also ration a commodity. For example, suppose the Bedford senior home had a limited number of covered parking spaces but alternative free parking in an adjacent lot. Suppose the rent for the covered stalls was $100 a month, and half were empty. The $100 price rationed the spaces to those willing to pay the high $100 price. The management could choose to reduce the rent, attracting more space renters until it filled. If the covered-space rent was set too low, the demand would exceed the spaces available. If the rent was set too high, the covered spaces would be partially unused. By adjusting the price (rent), the owner of the spaces can ration the supply to those willing and able to pay that price.

With the price at $100, those covered-space buyers who feel they need the space and can afford it are rationed the spaces. Those who say "I don't think it is worth it" will park outside in the uncovered adjacent lot. So price rationing forces supply and demand together at full or less than full use of the facility.

In the stock market, the price rations the shares available to those willing to pay the price. If some shares are taken off the market by companies buying their own shares, the rising price rations out the available remaining shares. Of course, unequal buying power in terms of wealth influences the demand, but demand is also influenced by personal choice. Price rations goods and services.

$ $

CHAPTER 16

$ $

The Economy and Unemployment

The state of the economy affects not only the attitude of investors toward various investments but also the returns on various investments and therefore their value. The US central bank has been assigned by Congress the dual goals of price stabilization (while encouraging 2 percent inflation) and the management of unemployment.

The US government publishes an unemployment rate monthly. The rate is the percent of unemployed of all those employed plus those looking for employment. They count only people who are over sixteen years old and exclude volunteers in employment and those not looking for work.

There exists what is termed a "natural rate of unemployment." In other words, there exists a rate—5 percent for example—that is natural. That the natural rate is above zero is due to unemployed people in transition between jobs, people recently but temporarily unemployed, recent school graduates, people recently released from military service, and those recently laid off. Should the unemployment rate go below the natural rate, it reflects a shortage of workers.

The price of labor needs to rise to bring supply and demand into balance. A shortage of labor would put upward pressure on wages, as employers cannot find employees. It would bid up the price of labor and pay overtime wages. So the Federal Reserve would like to keep unemployment at about the natural rate by influencing the availability of money and credit.

As with many statistics of the government, this rate is often misleading. It does not include as unemployed those who have given up trying find a job. To count as unemployed, they must be looking for work at the time. People who give up job-hunting and retire early, or just give up and look elsewhere for support, do not count as unemployed. As one would expect, it also pretty much ignores the homeless.

The rate also ignores those who are underemployed. By underemployed, we mean those who have taken a job below their qualification, usually because they could not find a job to fit their skills. And, of course, it excludes homemakers.

Of the US population of about 318,860,000 in 2015, only about half are considered the civilian labor force. The Bureau of Labor Statistics states that as of the end of June 2015, only 62.6 percent of the total labor force participated in the labor market; 37.4 percent did not. This participation rate declined from a high of 67.3 at the turn of the century (2000) to 62.6 percent in 2015. A low of 58.1 occurred in December 1954. Some of the decline in labor participation may be due to a gradual increase in the senior population.

CHAPTER 17

Inflation

If the things you bought in January required more money a period later, that is inflation. This is not always so easy to determine. Consider changing sizes: If you bought certain groceries on January 2014 for $100 and the same groceries were still $100 in 2015, you might think there was no price increase. However, perhaps the packages were 15 percent smaller. What you thought were the same grocery items at the same price were not the same. You may have noticed over the year that the packages had become smaller. People usually accept and visualize the nominal promised amounts and ignore the changes in the size of the package. To measure price change, you must compare the identical item from one year to the next.

The Consumer Price Index (CPI) calculated by the government is commonly used to measure inflation for consumers. The index includes prices of the same goods and services for a typical household from one period or year to the next. As some items are more important than others, varying weights are attached to the prices. For example, if toys are a larger item in consumer spending than clothing, that category receives a greater weight in calculating the CPI.

Food and energy prices are excluded from the CPI. The CPI is a weighted average of prices of the same basket of goods from one period to the next. This weighted-average index of consumer prices is compared to an initial year. To measure annual consumer inflation, you calculate the percentage increase in the CPI index for the year. If the index was 213 for the year 2015 and 225 for 2016, the ratio of the two indices is 225/213 or 1.056. Inflation would then be $(1.056 - 1.0) = .056$ or 5.6 percent. If the country was in a deflationary period, the change in prices would be negative.

The CPI is the measure used to adjust Social Security payments and many other economic and financial activities. If you received a 4 percent raise last year but the CPI rose 5.6 percent, you could buy less than you may have planned a year later: $5.6 - 4.0 = 1.6$ percent less. The purchasing power of your currency declined. Your real wage or perhaps real salary declined. By *real*, we mean the purchasing power of the currency/dollar. You believed you were gaining 4 percent in purchasing power, but it was an illusion. You actually lost 1.6 percent. Inflation means prices rise and purchasing power falls.

When prices begin to increase rapidly, the inflation is likely to be recognized by consumers. They are more likely to hoard items because they recognize that prices tomorrow are going likely to be higher than today. Spending accelerates, and it takes more money to buy an item each time they shop. This is termed *hyperinflation*. Consumers and businesses do not want to hold currency, so they spend it to get rid of it. They will not make investments that return the currency—no bonds, CDs, mortgages, and so on. These fail as stores of value as prices rise. Some corporations' common stock may survive if the company can raise its prices and revenue fast enough so that earnings and cash flow rise with inflation.

In the 1920s, the German paper currency, the mark, declined from 4 marks to one US dollar to 1,250,000,000 marks to one US dollar in just thirty months. This could be predicted years before it happened, as the money supply expanded—slowly at first and then rapidly.

To maintain the value or purchasing power of your savings during a high rate of inflation, investments should be made in hard assets not currency—actual physical things like gold, silver, real estate, farmland, even collectibles, which should increase in currency terms to maintain purchasing power. Investments that return paper money fall as prices rise. But in modest inflation, some companies will be able to respond quickly with price and revenue increases. Others will take time to adjust.

CHAPTER 18

Business and the Minimum Wage

Governments can rule a minimum wage to be paid for labor, rather than allowing demand in a free market to set wages. The politicians in government often argue that market wages are insufficient to provide a living income. Politicians do have the option of lowering income taxes for the lowest income brackets instead, if they have enough income. But raising the minimum wage raises income and income tax revenue for the governments.

An investor should understand the possible economic impact of raising the minimum wage, aside from the increase in personal income. Under the law, employers must pay the minimum wage for full-time employees. The rise in labor cost would have the immediate impact of reducing their profit (or increasing their loss). This might force some companies out of business, reducing employment. A business might favor hiring part-time employees over full-time employees in order to avoid the wage increase.

Assuming owners are not forced out of business, their cost of labor increases if the wage must rise by law. This will gradually change the owners' desired mix of labor and labor-saving equipment. The expected response of the owner would be to want to buy more labor-saving equipment and reduce the labor cost, the number of employees. Thus, raising the minimum wage can first reduce profits, but in the long run it will tend to reduce jobs and increase unemployment.

An alternative for the owner is to increase prices to raise revenue, offsetting the rise in the cost of labor. Raising prices has an inflationary impact, with its own effect on reducing the real incomes and spending ability of its customers. The ability to raise prices depends on the company's competitive situation. These impacts do not affect everyone equally.

Anytime the government decides to intercede in the free marketplace, it changes some aspect of the economy. Of course, many other changes impact the economy. Innovation has an impact. Imports of goods and services from abroad and exports to foreign consumers can have an impact. Changes in global currency values has an impact. Some of these may be desirable for employment and prices, and some may not.

CHAPTER 19

Politics and the Economy

Some people choose a career in politics. They are usually chosen to represent the members of a community—city, county, state, or nation. Ideally, they are selected when their views coincide with those they are to represent. But those seeking office can disguise their views. Outside of political skill, no other particular skill, education, experience, or training is necessary. But they do need to be popular and have a name familiarity with their constituency, among other attributes. Elections provide a lot of advertising.

The objective of the politician is to get elected. Politicians usually have a facility for effective speaking. Longevity in office develops experience in relations with other politicians. Most who plan to follow a political career are college graduates, with degrees frequently in law or political science. But others can be attracted to the position if they have name familiarity established in another field. Their actions can have huge impacts on the economy and investor decisions.

As in many social situations, the squeaky wheel gets the most grease—hence the increasing frequency of protest groups on public issues. Politicians may break election promises, but they may not successfully stay in office if they deviate very much from their own voters' views.

Politicians want to avoid unpopular decisions like reducing entitlement programs or raising taxes, despite overspending. The voting public will almost never support tough decisions, leading politicians to avoid difficult and restrictive issues.

Once a program is created and funded, it usually seeks to expand its own importance and budget. "Sunset" provisions that let the programs die after a fixed period are rare.

Public expenditures may be viewed by politicians to be costless, even though their spending may displace private capital investment and can lead to increasing debt and budget deficits. Their spending impacts various industries and investors' choices. Rising public demand for funds could push the price of capital upward, raising the capital cost for private use alternatives. Nationally, this may be temporarily avoided by borrowing abroad.

If infrastructure spending becomes popular, what happens to the common stock of companies who can benefit from more business in that field? If a robust military becomes popular, what happens to the common stock of companies in the defense business? What happens if gold is permitted to be an acceptable form of money? Those in politics can have a huge impact on various investment decisions. One had best keep abreast of those activities.

PART THREE

People and Their Investing Influence

CHAPTER 20

Selfish Investors

Our understanding of the influence of the mind on investment decisions asks for the motives behind this investment behavior. Do humans behave differently when confronted with investment decisions? Or is it just another facet human behavior- another form of self- preservation? Is the ego more important than money?

Cub Scouts and Boy Scouts influenced John in many ways when he was young. He recalls asking an elderly man if he could carry the man's groceries to the car. John said he was thanked by the man, and he felt good. Was John selfish for seeking that gratification?

Every human action or decision can be viewed as selfish. A man or woman does what he or she wants to do. If Fred buys groceries at the store, it is his choice. It is what Fred wants to do. Fred does that to eat, to sustain life and well-being, and/or to feel good.

If he gives money to a charity, it is because he wants to. He derives satisfaction from that. He is being selfish.

If Fred saves another person's life by pulling that person from a burning auto, he wants to avoid the distress of watching the person harmed or die. He wants the acclamation as a hero. Fred is being selfish.

If he saves some of his wages, he wants to provide for his future consumption. He is selfish.

If he gambles, he gets the thrill from the chance of winning. He is selfish.

If he works especially hard at his job for his employer, he wants a promotion or a raise. He is selfish.

Even if he wants to improve the material life of his family, he is selfish.

So if men, women, or children do what they want to do, aren't they selfish?

Now how about the peoples' government taxation? We don't want to give up part of our income to the government, but we pay because we want to avoid arrest and fines, or we want to help the government provide benefits. It is still selfish.

What about a criminal who breaks a government law? He does so because he wants to. The criminal is selfish. How about religion or the "church"? Are they unselfish? No, they too are selfish. They take actions that are most beneficial to them, monetarily or otherwise.

Everyone is selfish. Everyone does what he or she wants to do. Different people want different things.

Obviously, our actions are affected by the *mores* of society. Giving is good. Saving a life is good. Protecting the family or the country is good.

Society has a different meaning of the term *selfish*. A man who does things for himself, his family, or some group can be viewed as being selfish, while doing things for someone else or a group or giving up something he controls may be regarded as unselfish. Society is the judge in the court of selfishness.

Society's mores can mutate/change over time. For example, society's view of gay marriage and society's view of a man and woman living together outside of marriage can change. Many social mores are written into law. Could society's view of what is selfish also change? Everyone may not have the same opinion of what that means.

Buying and selling common stock are selfish actions because the buyers get what they want by paying the necessary price for ownership. Sellers want cash and get what they want. The trade is a selfish win-win.

Some choose to volunteer or make donations because that grants personal satisfaction. You agree that people are different. But humans do what they want to do and are thus selfish.

$ $

CHAPTER 21

$ $

Greed

Greed is a term usually associated with money or wealth. It is usually seen as a negative characteristic. A person may be considered greedy if he or she already has wealth but wants more. People may even be labeled greedy if they are not wealthy but behave aggressively to achieve wealth. It can happen when a person becomes well off or rich but wants to become wealthier.

This behavior can become a habit or often be addictive. Some people cannot stop accumulating money or wealth. They are regarded as especially greedy if they use shady or unpopular methods to achieve wealth or income. It's like a game to some, with one's net worth as the score.

We should be careful if we want to transfer this description to every company's behavior. Publicly owned companies, as distinguished from private companies, have many owners and shareholders who may be neither rich nor greedy. It is the company's responsibility to its owners to see to it that the company maximizes its profit opportunities within the rules of fair play. And private companies will have a profit responsibility to their principals.

However, some companies can be seen as greedy. They may have some degree of monopoly power and can try to influence the spending of segments of the population and government. In this respect, former President Eisenhower warned of military-industrial power and influence.

Even if a company has a single owner, it may be difficult to describe the owner as greedy if his or her objective is to see the company succeed. The owner's company can be providing access to a valuable product or service to its customers. Its success can be a win for not only the company but also its owners and customers. It is up to the company to find or discover what consumers want before it can be successful.

Greed is a characteristic usually regarded by society as undesirable. It is not so easy to identify in practice, and it is not easy to control.

$ $

CHAPTER 22

$ $

Incentives

Some investors have a desire to preserve or increase their nest egg to build a retirement fund, a child's education fund, or perhaps funds for future purchases. They have an incentive to achieve their goals perhaps by investing in common stock and/or other alternatives.

An incentive is the carrot in the saying about the carrot and the stick. The carrot is the reward for the desired behavior. In training a pet dog, one uses food or a snack as the incentive for the dog to be potty-trained. People rationally respond to personal incentives. The incentive may be a job promotion, a raise in pay, or a bonus. This will work for an individual or a family, the incentive being greater income. The family breadwinner may want more days of vacation, a key to the executive washroom, a membership in a club, a bouquet of flowers, or a star on his or her record.

Incentives are as key to life as a bone is to a dog. Incentives may also be a key to the advancement or success of a group, a company, an organization, or a team. Some incentives can cause a Girl Scout troop to want to sell more cookies. Incentives bring about selfish behavior.

Income taxes can dull the incentives to inventors and entrepreneurs, as the reward for innovation is reduced. Lack of a sufficient reward can reduce motivation. High taxes or other restrictions may cause the creator or innovator to go elsewhere by immigrating to another country with lower taxes. A country with central planners who make all the economic decisions reduces the incentives available, limiting freedom of choice and discouraging improvement and innovation. Incentives are crushed.

If the so-called "carrot" is removed, the only way to stimulate behavior is the "stick." In this case, that is the punishment for not behaving the planners' way. Punishment can also be fees, fines, taxes, or lack of patent, trademark, or copyright protections.

High income taxes and an excess of rules or regulations can frustrate the ambitions of those seeking the rewards of success. Taxing dividends, capital gains, and the sale/merger of the entire company reduces the returns—the incentives. Patents and copyright laws are important to innovation and company value.

High property taxes can produce strange consequences. A tax on the number of windows in a house will reduce windows in construction, a tax on the square feet of a building will reduce size, and so on. A wealth tax can also reduce incentives to save. It may cause the movement of capital abroad. Thus a nation or even a state without incentives will tend toward stagnation. If a country, state, or region wants economic growth, it provides the incentives to bring about innovation and entrepreneurship. States and cities may create incentives to attract jobs. Incentives seek to bring about a desired behavior.

$ $

CHAPTER 23

$ $

Inequality

My neighbor south of me buys a new car about every other year. Although that sounded nice, I was not sure how he was able to afford it. We'd confessed on one occasion that we both had about the same income. It just seemed that my wife and I wanted to spend differently than he and his wife did. I think he collected watches and his wife shoes. My wife was big on charity causes. I liked to travel. People choose different consumption patterns. And, of course, inequality in wealth or income—whether from inheritance, luck, saving, or successful investments—will likely exhibit different choices.

Although it's not true of everyone, many want what others have. There seems to be a belief that all Americans should have a car, a house, a doctor, a telephone, a television, and so on. The poor should not be poor, and it is thought to be the government's task to bring that about. The cry for such a "living wage" seems to grow.

Many socialists believe equality should be the goal. But over the decades of life and history, there has always been a lowest-income population and a highest-income group. Income inequality may be due to different skills, personalities, inheritance, training, and education. It may be just chance that one's abilities are in more demand, causing increased wages. Inequality is inescapable.

A way to eliminate income inequality would be to tax people 100 percent of their assets and income and redistribute it equally. If this were to happen, people would not be paid according to their efforts or abilities.

The human desire for gain would likely lead to stealing from others. In such a state, there would be no monetary incentives. What would be the advantage of working hard? What would be the incentive for saving and investing or training? In the absence of differences in income, one might possibly observe a quest for power and/or perhaps just respect. Differences exist.

Communism and socialism (the command economies) control the capital and therefore must plan its distribution. They try to achieve income equality within a country, but even they failed to eliminate inequality entirely. The leading elite and a few selected skilled individuals identified by the state become the high-income class, although the higher income might not always be in salary. But for most, the ability to reach a higher income is not available. Output and quality of work usually are not rewarded.

People are different. They have different genes. They have different ambitions, different aptitudes, different incentives and abilities. Inequality exists from birth. Shorty will never play center in basketball. Some people are hard workers; some are social climbers; some are politicians; some are leaders. Some are savers and investors, but some are followers, not savers and investors. Some are rich, and some are poor. Some companies are large, and some are small. Some companies are publicly owned, and some are private. Inequality is inevitable in humanity.

CHAPTER 24

Diversity

Imagine that one country—in the interests of efficiency and cost reduction—decreed that only one type of automobile would be produced for the entire nation. Everyone who did have a car had an identical car. There was no attempt to respond to different tastes. There was no variety in shapes, functions, or colors. The only choice was to have a car or not have a car. Perhaps everyone would select a car over no car. But there would be trouble in the parking lot. In any case, we would expect all this to reduce the desire for a car.

Would you rather have a variety of flowers or just one flower? Would you rather see everyone looking identical or unique? Would you find it boring if everyone thought exactly as you thought? Certainly, companies are not identical. Thank goodness, we have diversity.

Diversity in cars, in flowers, in looks, in gender, in generations, in investments, in religion, and in thought ought to be celebrated. Diversity in languages, race, food, politics, likes, and dislikes makes for a more interesting life for all. The alcoholic beverage of choice may be beer in Prague and Berlin, but it's wine in Paris and Rome.

The incentive to travel is often based on diversity—an opportunity to observe different cultures and ways of living. Travel would likely be much less common if it were not for diversity. Diversity is desirable and appreciated. So should then be diversity in skin color and religion.

In the stock market, there exists common stock in many different companies, industries, regions, and countries. To protect this diversity, society must seek some common ground for behavior. To live together in diversity, we need some rules for coexistence.

Society has provided mores to guide human behavior. Mores are social guidelines, like shaking hands when introduced or holding the door open for someone coming behind. Diverse religions also provide some rules for behavior, "do not steal," "do not kill," and "do not commit adultery" are *mores* advanced by religion and codified by law. National leaders may also provide rules, even though there are differences in governance. World organizations seek to provide rules like protecting sovereignty, peace, trade, and currency.

But diversity in most things is treasured. Certainly, common stock investment offers a huge pool of investment alternatives, different in one aspect or another. These can be used to reduce risk in investment, as they are not identical in their changes in value. There are bonds, common stock, preferred stock, notes, REITs, ETFs, mutual funds, closed-end funds, mortgages, and CDs, to name a few.

PART FOUR

Some Errors of the Mind in Investing

$ $

CHAPTER 25

$ $

The Money Illusion

For $100, I bought a one-year 3 percent certificate of deposit (CD) from my bank on January 1, 2014, that promised to pay me $103 in one year. Great! A gain of $3.

What I did not observe was that the price for my basket of goods had crept up by 5 percent during the same year, 2014. That was 5 percent inflation for me. At the end of the year, my $103 bought fewer good and services.

With the 5 percent increase in prices of goods and services, the $3 gain from my CD was an illusion. The real return was 3 percent – 5 percent = a loss of 2 percent in purchasing power. The bank paid me the $3, which was what I expected, but it was a false gain. The $3 interest paid me was not enough to buy the same goods a year later. I could buy 10 apples on January 1, 2014, but only 9.8 apples a year later. The creep in prices from day to day was so small as not to be noticeable.

I also bought a bond that promised to pay me 5 percent every year on my $1,000 investment. In other words, I planned on a 5 percent yield, or $50 a year. But I did not notice that prices were rising by 5 percent a year. My 5 percent return was an illusion. In reality, I was paid nothing. I thought I had gained by buying the bond, but I did not. I had no gain in purchasing power.

This so-called investment returned me nothing. The real return was zero. I even paid the government a tax on the $5 of interest income, so I lost.

This illustration can also be applied to wages and salaries. A 2 percent raise can be seen as an increase, but if purchasing power declines by 2 percent, the raise is an illusion.

Money illusion might be called a human disease. Investors should look for reality. The difficulty for investors is that they cannot forecast the change in purchasing power of their currency. Still, they can have expectations. Saving for future consumption by investing is a very difficult task, especially under unstable or questionable economic conditions.

Typically, yields or returns will adjust eventually to compensate for expected inflation. A nominal interest rate may present just a money illusion. It is not real. A 5 percent promise to pay may include a 2 percent compensation for expected inflation so that the real return is only 3 percent. The 5 percent is an illusion.

CHAPTER 26

$ $

Introspection

My mother pointed out to me the Golden Rule: We should treat others as we wish to be treated. This was helpful as a guideline for social behavior. I would try to understand actions of others by looking to my own behavior if I was in their circumstances. I was to visualize my behavior as if I were in their shoes.

Introspection is like putting yourself in another person's position and looking at something from their point of view. Many of us forget to use introspection when discussing or arguing a cause, a behavior, or the actions of others. Our view of the world is not universal, not everyone's. No one person sees the world exactly as others see it. To understand another, it is important to look at the world from his or her point of view. But it is not always easy. A man, recently divorced, may have a very different outlook on romance than his happily married friend. A mother who lost a daughter will have a different view of her life than a mother who still has her daughter. A coal miner will likely have a very different view of life than an airline pilot.

A lawyer can be expected to look at things differently than a psychologist. They may have great difficulty agreeing on ways to treat a lawbreaker. The lawyer will look to the law, and the psychologist will likely look at behavioral background. The psychologist may try to understand the behavior by putting himself in the lawbreaker's shoes. Perhaps the lawbreaker had an abusive childhood. Or perhaps she was spoiled by her parents and became accustomed to getting whatever she wanted.

Introspection may help one understand behavior of others even though the behavior may not be acceptable to another or against the law. Remember—we are all different and appreciate differences and diversity. Do other buyers in the stock market think exactly as I think? If they did, then when I want to buy a stock, others should also think that way. Who would be selling? —unless they just need cash.. Minds do not always mirror others' thinking.

$ $

CHAPTER 27

$ $

Mirror Thinking

Some investors use the term *mirror thinking* for introspection, as if you were looking in the mirror for how to behave. If I like ice cream, I expect you and everyone else to like ice cream. Doesn't everyone like ice cream? That may be a wrong assumption. These investors forget about human diversity. Mirror thinking does not always provide the right choice for behavior.

Even heads of state can make serious errors by assuming the head of XYZ country values the same goals as SOA. A punishment or reward by XYZ for its behavior is likely to fail in its influence on SOA.

If SOA country put tariffs (taxes) on all goods the United States is trying to sell in SOA, the price would have to be set high enough to pay the tariff as well as the cost of the goods transported. Suppose the United States puts a tariff or tax on Iranian carpets being offered for sale in the United States. The US retail seller must put a price on the carpet that will pay not only the Iranian cost but also the tariff collected for the US government. The higher price caused by the tariff will reduce demand in the United States. Carpets coming to the United States from another country with no tariff.or those produced in the United States will sell better, having that selling advantage. Thus the Iranian company's profit will be less because of reduced sales.

But suppose the head of state does not give a hoot if the Iranian carpet company does not sell carpets in the United States? He does not think that way. All the Iranian head of state cares about is power or influence over other countries. The heck with its profit-seeking companies.

If CDX invades ESC the United States may want to stop the invasion. Not wanting to use a military option, the United States refuses to sell goods to CDX and freezes CDX peoples' bank accounts in the US. But the CDX leaders are not bothered by these sanctions. They have other objectives, like having more power over others by capturing ESC.

Buyers and sellers participating in the stock market must not expect all others to view stock value as they do. Relying on introspection or mirror thinking could lead to unexpected decisions. These differences in value opinion may bring about trades.

$ $
# CHAPTER 28
$ $
Extrapolation

In an extended discussion, my friend and I argued about the price of residential real estate, specifically single-family homes. In 2007, my friend said he had found that the median price of single-family homes had risen every year for the past eleven years. He wanted me to partner with him to buy a home as an investment, finance it with a mortgage, and rent it out. He did buy a home, and by 2011, it was valued by a realtor at 20 percent less than he paid for it.

What was yesterday is supposed to continue to today. People expect the past to continue in the future. This is human nature. Extrapolation is the use of the recent past to project the future. If my friend had drawn a chart of median prices over recent years, he could likely visualize the future rise in price.

Suppose I draw a chart for the price of gasoline every day for two weeks. Every day, the price is higher than the previous day. What is your estimate of the price tomorrow, up or down? Usually up, of course. Suppose the X cell phone has added more features every year for fifteen years. Do you think next year's cell phone will have more features or fewer?

Suppose the cost of a new forty-inch television has fallen every year for seven years. Do you think the same television will cost more next year? No; you expect the price will continue to fall. In all these examples, the prediction is a continuation of the prior periods behavior.

But of course, many patterns of behavior do not follow a steady or a constant change in the same direction. That is true for stock-price movements as well. Market prices on the Standard & Poor's 500 often will fluctuate as they move in an up or down direction. If a company's earnings have increased every year for the past five years by an average of 7 percent, one could expect a continuation of earnings growth of about 7 percent.

It is natural for humans to extrapolate, but directions or trends can change. When they do change, we may be surprised or even make a costly error. Use caution when extrapolating. It is a human weakness to always expect the future to be a continuation of the past.

$ $
# CHAPTER 29
$ $
Loss Aversion

A trait investors often have is sticking to an investment even when the market value has declined since purchase. Investors tend to not want to surrender the investment and realize a loss. They hang on in anticipation or hope of recovery, even in the face of declining demand for the investment. They do not wish to recognize their mistake or the change in conditions that caused the decline. They do not want to realize the loss.

This is a human tendency to avert the final decision to realize a loss. They hang on and on as the stock price declines, each day not wanting to sell, in the hope that it will rise again tomorrow. The tendency to avoid recognizing a loss is called *loss aversion*, and it can lead to catastrophe.

In the stock market, investors can provide for an escape from the wishful nvestment decision with the use of stop orders—or better yet, trailing stop orders—placed with their broker or agent. Once placed, the stop order removes the emotion of not wanting to realize a loss. The investor avoids a decision, as the stop order takes the decision out of the investor's control.

Suppose an investor buys five hundred shares of Tribute at $50 a share, in expectation of a future gain. A month later, the price declines to $48 a share, then the following month to $45 a share, then $43 a share, and then $40. Ouch! The investor hates to sell at $45, at $43, and then at $40, hoping that tomorrow will be better. A stop order would instruct the sale of the five hundred shares under prescribed conditions.. If the order was to sell if the price to fell to $45 or 10 percent decline, a sell order would be entered when the price fell to $45. This would remove emotion from the decision.

If, instead, the price rose after the purchase at $50 a share, to $55 and then $60, the investor would want to move his stop order up to partially protect the gain. Better yet, he could enter a "10 percent trailing stop" at $50. In that case, if it declined 10 percent, the instruction would be to enter a sell order. If, however, the price rose to $60 a share, the trailing stop moved to 10 percent below $60, or $54. The investor would not have to manually move the stops. In placing stop orders, the investor wants to allow for routine dips in the price without being sold out. A 15 or 25 percent trailing stop might be more appropriate for a more volatile stock.

The investor who has selected shares of a company that he or she wants to hold for the long, long run and may decide to just ride out declines in a bear (declining) market. Alternatively, the investor may even decide to seize the opportunity to add shares at the lower price, decreasing the average cost of all shares held.

$ $
# CHAPTER 30
$ $
Idle Funds

Another condition that often exists for the stock market investor is the annoying state of mind surrounding a cash balance. The investor believes that all funds should be working. Given that belief, the investor looks for something to reduce or eliminate the cash balance. Instead of waiting to invest in a value opportunity, the attitude is to look for any stock that has a chance to provide a positive return.

Suppose Pete has a brokerage account that is invested in the shares of four companies. He invested an amount he felt comfortable with in each promising company. But he had an $11,000 cash balance remaining. After a period of time, seeing the idle balance, he stretched to find another company to complete his portfolio making all funds employed. Nothing came along. Finally, he lowered his standard and invested this amount in something that was okay but nothing to be enthused about. Bad move!

An investment in cash can be a wise choice, for it provides an ability to select a new exciting opportunity when it comes along without selling one or part of his four investments. He felt he could always sell his bad move, but at some expense—at least the buy and sell transaction costs, even if he sells at the same price he paid. By investing idle funds in this manner, the investor surrenders the ability to respond to a new opportunity without disturbing the rest of his portfolio. Even selling the idle-funds investment incurs not only a selling cost and perhaps a loss.

$ $

CHAPTER 31

$ $

Normalcy Bias

Another consideration in managing a stock investment is a reliance on a stock price to have a normal range of fluctuation. After a time, the range will be viewed as "normal" behavior. A decline in price outside this range might be wrongly ignored as a random exception to the range—an outlier, as a statistician would say. A larger than normal price decline might be viewed with the expectation that the price will return to its normal range, and sometimes it does. The bias is the misplaced confidence that it will do so consistently. In other words, human behavior tends to place excess weight on a return to normal.

Suppose the Trinity stock, owned by Felix for the past twenty-seven months, has traded on the exchange between 27 and 31, so that it rises and falls between 27 and 31 occur month after month. Now Felix sees a price of 25. Is this the sign of a real change in the outlook for the company, or is it just an anomaly? Normalcy bias means that Felix favors the view that it is a rare event—and the price should return to normal, meaning 27 plus rather than a change in the Trinity stock outlook.

If this is expected to be a long-term investment, the investor could consider creating a moving average (MA) of prices to try to determine a trend. A twenty-day MA is created by taking the average of the closing price of the stock for the last twenty trading days and then continuing to move that average by taking the daily average of twenty prices after dropping the oldest price and adding the latest price. You can produce a series of twenty-day stock-price averages when you chart the series over time. This tends to smooth the fluctuations and help with identifying price trends.

You might want to add bands about this MA that display a range of routine fluctuation. The deviation from bands (like Bollinger bands) around the twenty-day MA should identify prices outside the normal range. Outliers or prices outside a normal range should challenge the investor to look for causes of the price behavior before continuing to be confident in the investment. Was there news? Was there an earnings surprise, a change of management, or a decline in debt rating?

PART FIVE

Some Common Investment Alternatives

$ $
# CHAPTER 32
$ $
Stock Options

An option to buy a common stock is called a *call option*. If you were to buy a call option on Bubbles common stock, you would own a contract that gives you the right, but not an obligation, to buy one hundred shares of Bubbles at a specified price called the *strike price* or the *exercise price* for a fixed period of time. Just buying the call contract gives you leverage. You can control the one hundred shares using a call option with a much smaller investment than buying the actual shares. But if the stock price never reaches the strike price by the expiration date, the call is worthless.

If Bubbles stock is offered at $65, it would cost you $6,500 (plus a commission fee) to own the hundred shares. If the stock price rose to $75 in six months on the sale of your shares, you would gain $1,000, or about 15 percent, on the $6,500 investment.

Instead, assume you invested (bought) in one call contract (which is for one hundred shares) for $100 with a strike price of $70 for six months and exercised the call to gain a $75 stock. Then you sold the shares for $7,500, which returned you a profit of $500 ($7,500 – $7,000). Subtract the call price of $100 for a gain of $400 on the $100 investment, or 400 percent. A 400 percent gain is better than a 15 percent gain. You levered your $100.for a gain of $500 -$100=$400.

This example assumes no transaction fees, which, of course, reduce the gain. But it does demonstrate the leverage possibilities of a call option, which controls one hundred shares with fewer dollars. It is also important to note that if Bubbles' share price did not climb above $70, the call option would be worthless at expiration, and you lost the $100.

American-style options allow you to exercise them any time up until expiration. European-style options can only be exercised or not at expiration.

Instead of buying a call, one may also sell (or write) a call. This contract requires the writer to deliver the stock for the exercise price, if so requested by the owner of the contract. If the shares are selling in the market at less than the strike price, the owner will not choose to exercise the call, and the writer will keep the option premium paid by the buyer.

If the shares are selling at more than the exercise price, the buyer of the contract may ask that the shares be delivered at the exercise price—or the option might just be sold. The call at its higher value in the option market would be *in the money* before expiration. Buyers of call options expect share prices to rise in the stock market.

Some may just sell/write calls as a way to augment income from the collection of call premiums. If the share price does not rise during the option period, the writer/seller keeps the call premium.

Writing a call is one way to sell your shares and receive more than the current selling price, because of the premium received. If the writer already owns the shares to deliver, he does not need to purchase them. The writing of the call is then called a *covered call*. If the seller/writer sells the option without owning the shares, then it's a *naked call*.

Another option contract is called a *put*. A put option gives the buyer of the put contract the right to sell shares of the company at the strike or exercise price. Those who buy puts either expect the share prices to fall. The buyer of the put provides insurance against a price decline, for the cost of the put option.

Assume Donna owns a hundred shares of TXRC, which she paid at $7. Donna has held the shares for some time, and the share price has risen to $16/share. If she is later expecting a decline in TXRC's share price, she could buy a put at an exercise price of $14 as a way to guarantee at least $14. This way, she can keep the shares, but she has insurance against market decline below $14. This insurance cost is the option premium.

Ted, as the writer/seller of the put, is interested in buying shares of this company, but at a lower price than $16. He sells a put with a strike price of $13. If TXRC stock price declines to $13, the put option holder exercises the put, he has to buy 100 shares at $13. But he obtains the shares at a lower price than $16. The put seller may be trying to augment income by selling puts and predicts the share prices will not decline enough to require him to buy shares. If TXRC's price in the share market declines to $15 at or near the expiration of the put, Ted just pockets the option premium as added income, for it will not be exercised. If TXRC's price declines below $13, he has to buy those shares at $13,.

Another investor, Pete, expects price stability, so he sells calls and puts for income. If, on the other hand, Pete expected extreme volatility in prices but was unsure which way they would go, he could buy a put and a call (a straddle) and look forward to a lot of price fluctuations to gain enough on one of the options to pay for both by exercising one of them for a gain.

Options offer a much wider group of alternative strategies of investing in common stock combined with options. This is not a promotion of the use of options by the investor. Be careful, as one can also lose money fast—leverage creates high percentage losses as well gains.

$ $

CHAPTER 33

$ $

Currencies

Currency is money. It is used as an item of exchange for goods or services, payment of debt, and investment. In the United States, the currency is the dollar. In Russia, it is the ruble. In Japan, it is the yen. In Europe, it is the euro. In Great Britain, it is the pound (sterling). In China, it is the yuan or renminbi, and in Switzerland, it is the franc. An effective currency requires confidence by the citizens in its acceptance in exchange and as a store of value. A lack of confidence destroys currency's usefulness.

Each currency has a different value in terms of another currency. As of this writing, a Swiss franc can buy .96 dollars and 1.04 euros. Its relation to other currencies is largely determined by its relative purchasing power and the country's interest rates. Higher interest rates relative to others increase the demand for the high interest rate currency, all else the same.

A Swiss franc (as distinguished from a French franc) has different purchasing power than the Russian ruble. Thus, for each pair of currencies, there is an exchange rate. The US dollar can buy so many rubles and a different number of euros. There are many, many exchange rates. You could construct a whole matrix, a table, of exchange rates, like the small sample below:

	Dollar	Euro	Yen	Pound	S Franc
Dollar	1.00	1.09	.0081	1.56	1.04
Euro	.92	1.00	.0074	1.44	.96
Yen	124.00	135.00	1.00	194.00	130.00
Pound	.64	.70	.0057	1.00	.67
S Franc	.96	1.04	.0077	1.49	1.00

In the first row, we can see how many dollars it takes to buy one euro ($1.09), one yen ($.0081), one pound ($1.56), and one Swiss franc($1.04). In the first column, we can see how much of the other currencies we can get for one dollar. Each rate in the table is called a *cross rate*. If I travel to Japan, I will need their local currency, the yen, for purchases in Japan. I plan to trade $1 for 124 yen, and $100 will buy me 12,400 yen.

In international commerce, if you wish to buy a Japanese Nissan auto, you would expect to pay for the Nissan in yen. You would need to ask a bank or other foreign exchange dealer to exchange your dollars for yen to make payment. There is a market for currencies to facilitate such transactions: the Forex (foreign exchange) market. In this particular case, the Nissan company in Japan sends cars to the auto dealer through an importer in the United States who takes care of the currency exchange for you, so you just pay dollars to make the purchase.

If the dollar/yen exchange rate were to change so that it takes more dollars to buy yen, you could expect that the price of the car in dollars will also rise. Changes in exchange rates impact the volume and nature of trade and both the country's economies. Given competitors in other countries, it can change the trade and economies of all countries by changing the whole matrix of currencies.

Currency wars may exist when countries seek to improve their trade status by reducing the value of their currency. Making their currency cheaper by devaluation makes their goods cheaper to other countries, increasing the export business of the devaluing country.

There exist a few currencies in the world that are used by most countries as a rainy-day fund or monetary reserves. These are the currencies that are accepted as payment in international trade and used as reserves for the country's banking systems. These include the US dollar, the euro, and, to a lesser extent, the Swiss franc, Japanese yen, Chinese renminbi, Canadian dollar, and Australian dollar. These currencies are called *reserve currencies*. The US dollar is currently the dominant reserve currency.

The Forex market is the largest financial market in the world. It is where currencies are bought and sold. As of today, all oil is priced in US dollars, and countries most often hold US dollars as reserves.

The watchdog of these currencies around the world and promoter of stable currencies to facilitate trade is the International Monetary Fund (IMF). It has the power to lend money (a bundle of reserve currencies) to a country to help stabilize its currency, usually in exchange for economic reforms. This would hopefully restore confidence in the country's currency. The IMF also has the power to approve reserve currencies. China is one of the largest economies in the world, and recently its currency, the yuan/renminbi, was added to the list of reserve currencies.

$ $

CHAPTER 34

$ $

Banking

A bank or credit union will hold your money in a savings account or checking account. It accepts deposits to either account. A savings account is also called a *time deposit*. The bank could ask for time before releasing money back to the depositor. Usually, banks do not require a delay in releasing the money back to the depositor, but they could. For large amounts, they are more likely to delay the release of funds. A certificate of deposit(CD) stipulates a fixed period before release of the funds back to the depositor without a penalty.

A checking account is a demand deposit. The balance in the account is payable on demand by the account holder. A check is just a promise to pay; it actually takes time to collects the funds promised on the check deposit from the bank of the check writer. Thus, release of funds could be delayed for a limited period, arguing that it takes time for collection of funds from the issuing bank. Any deposit becomes the property of the bank, which provides you with an IOU for the amount of the deposit.

The bank realizes from experience that it does not have to hold 100 percent of the funds on deposit, ready to meet demand. It is unlikely that every depositor will make claims on their entire balance of the account at the same time. Surely, that will not happen. Therefore, the bank can loan some of the money to individuals, companies, and governments for a fee—an interest rate.

Banks lend by granting a deposit to the borrower. The bank will lend several times the amount of its own funds set aside (as reserves) to meet demands. The bank can profit as long as the interest it receives from loans and investments exceeds its cost of operation and the interest cost it must pay depositors. Thus, the financial institution acts as an intermediary between borrowers and lenders, and its operating revenue depends on the spread between the rate it lends and the rate it pays.

Lending out all the money it receives in deposits would be foolish; it must keep some cash to meet demands of account holders who wish cash/currency. Therefore, banks hold some funds to meet cash demands and checks written by depositors. In fact, state and federal regulators require a certain percentage of deposits be held as reserves.

Problems for the bank can arise with poor lending practices, resulting in defaults on its loans, leading to losses. Losses could then lead to lack of confidence by deposit account holders that their IOU (deposit) is safe and will be paid in cash on demand. Concern arises about the ability of the bank to meet demands. Panic can arise as account holders rush to take their money out of the bank. Banks' fractional reserves do involve some risk to depositors.

The history of fractional reserve banking throughout the world has demonstrated that economic emergencies can lead to heavy demands for currency. Banks can be caught unprepared, with limited reserves. Demand-deposit account holders can lose confidence that the bank will be able to meet all demands. To prevent this loss of confidence and bank runs, banks buy insurance for their accounts. In the United States, the federal government created the Federal Deposit Insurance Corporation to provide account insurance for commercial banks.

The FDIC fund, at this writing, insures about $9.3 trillion in deposits with a $25 billion fund, or less than 1 cent on the dollar. Credit Unions have a similar fund, the NCUSIF. The availability of central banks like the Federal Reserve allows an individual bank to borrow reserves in order to meet unexpected demands. Most of the banks' reserves are held as deposits with the central bank. When the reserve drops below the legal requirement, the bank can borrow from the Fed Res at an interest rate, called the *discount rate*, to meet its reserve requirement.

The Federal Reserve is also asked by law to influence the economy in favor of a stable (or a slowly increasing) price level and reduce unemployment to a natural level. Its tools include the ability to change the money supply by buying or selling US Treasury bonds and bills from or to banks to change bank reserves, which limit or expand the lending or investment by banks. It can also change the interest rate (the discount rate) the Fed charges in lending reserves to a bank. The Fed could also change banks' reserve requirement, but that has been rare.

For example, say the Federal Reserve buys a $1,000 Treasury bond from Security Bank, paying for the bond by increasing Security Bank's deposit (reserves) with the Fed. This deposit increases Security Bank's reserves by $1,000. Given the bank reserve requirement of 20 percent, the bank can now increase its deposits by $5,000, by lending or investing $5,000. When Micah comes to Security Bank for a construction loan, the bank grants him a $5,000 loan in the form of a deposit. As deposits rise, money supply increases, because the definition of money supply includes cash plus bank deposits.

The banking system can play an important role in impacting inflation, unemployment, and the earnings of publicly owned companies. The bank may even lend directly to investors in the stock market.

$ $

CHAPTER 35

$ $

Insurance

The terms *certainty, risk,* and *uncertainty* should be defined. Certainty is an outcome of an event that is known for sure. For example, if you drop a ball, we know for certain, on Earth, that the ball will fall. If it rains, something will get wet. There are a lot more events where the outcomes are so highly expected that we call them certain, like turning on a light, flushing a toilet, picking a flower, or starting a car.

Risk is the likelihood of each of the known outcomes of the event. The probability or likelihood of getting a head on a flip of a coin is one half, or 50 percent. The probability of a specific number on a roll of an honest die is one sixth. There exist many events where the odds of different outcomes are virtually known that we can still call the event risky.

Uncertainty is when the various outcomes of an event and/or their likelihood are unknown. There exist many degrees of uncertainty—very uncertain, somewhat uncertain, and so on. The future price of a common share is uncertain.

Let's say Active Insurance Co. enters into a contract with you to pay your spouse $100,000 when you die. To Active Insurance, there is a lot of uncertainty about when it will have to pay a specific death claim. How much should it charge for that potential liability? The charge is called a *premium.*

History tells us the average number of deaths in each year. The number of deaths of fifty-year-olds is fairly predictable. An uncertain event is just a risky event as a result of pooling of a large number of very similar events. Experience tells a company like Active that an average number of deaths for fifty-one-year-olds is three per thousand, age fifty-two is five per thousand, and so on. This determines the total number of death claims the company expects to pay each year. These life expectancy tables, based on experience and what the company expects to earn on any investment, determine the amount of the periodic premium to charge. This is the basis of life insurance.

Fire insurance, auto insurance, and medical insurance depend on similar pooling to determine the average or expected claims and therefore the premium the company must charge. Insurance is based on pooling events to reduce uncertainty in order to get predictable or risky results.

Bank deposits are pooled and insured by the FDIC to provide confidence in the banking system. Balances in stockbrokerage accounts are also insured. Of course, as with any insurance, the insurer must have large numbers of insureds to give reasonable confidence in the amount of claims in each period. Insurance companies become popular investments themselves through their company shares.

$ $

CHAPTER 36

$ $

Precious Metals

Often, one component for those advocating financial allocation is a recommendation to invest 5 or 10 percent of their investments in a precious metal. These include gold, silver, and occasionally others like platinum, diamonds, and palladium. However, the latter are rarely used, for the market for diamonds and palladium is not as liquid nor do they have a wealth of history in the role for crisis support. Here, we are speaking of gold and silver bullion or bullion coins—and not coins in a numismatic sense, where rare coins become collectable, but in a commodity sense.

Both gold and silver have a long history as a safe haven in times of financial crisis. In times of inflation, loss of confidence in the currency, extreme uncertainty, excessive debt, or lack of faith in financial institutions, gold and silver are sought to perform the function of money—a medium of exchange and/or a store of value. They are also often sought after to offset losses in other investments to help stabilize the total value of the portfolio. In many periods in the past, these metals were used as the primary form of money. Sometimes mining interests have pressured lawmakers for their use as money to maintain demand and price of the metal.

Gold and silver holdings generate no dividends or interest and thus are not reportable for income tax purposes, unless you realize a capital gain. They are not active assets that produce income like businesses, thus there is little love for having gold and silver as a large portion of a portfolio.

Some investors pay attention to the gold/silver ratio—the price of gold divided by the price of silver. A ratio of 50 means it costs fifty ounces of silver to buy one ounce of gold. But the ratio varies wildly over time. When both silver and gold are used as a precious metal money, the ratio serves to say when one or the other is cheap or expensive to the followers. Those who depend on the ratio know that if the ratio is very high, silver is cheap. Silver should be the less expensive alternative to use as a crisis safeguard.

As of November 2015, the ratio was about 75. This means that silver is cheap. The average ratio during the twentieth century was 47.50, and the ratio at the beginning of the twenty-first century was about 54. The long-term average before 1900 was 16. The investor is not advised to place much faith in the gold/silver ratio.

During times of inflation or expected inflation, both gold and silver values can rise dramatically. In any economic/financial crisis, they can bolster the value stability of the allocated full portfolio and again increase in price because of uncertainty sounding investing alternatives.

$ $

CHAPTER 37

$ $

Gold

Gold is a precious metal that has been regarded as money in exchange and as a store of value for centuries. Silver has also been regarded as a money, but gold seems to have the edge in investor confidence. Money is usually defined as something that is generally accepted in exchange for goods and services, as a unit of measure (as in pricing), as a standard of deferred payment (as in a mortgage or annuity), and as a store of value (like a savings account).

Today, specially printed paper is used as money. The bills are printed as a promise to pay by the Federal Reserve, the central bank of the United States. In earlier days, paper dollars were a promise to pay in gold or silver at an official rate set by the government. The paper was easier to carry around and store than the actual gold or silver metal or even coins. Paper money is supplied to the economy at the discretion of the central bank with the help of the commercial banking system. They are the managers of the money system. At times, they feed a lot money into the economy, pushing interest rates down, in hopes that it will stimulate economic activity by allowing increasing loans and investments by commercial banks.

Gold for many years past was a suitable form of money, for it was rare, durable, and portable. Paper too is durable, portable, and relativity rare, but only at the discretion of the central bank. Gold could be used to create coins, which was helpful in an exchange economy, as it did not need to be weighed and tested for purity for each transaction. The use of gold bullion and gold coins as money kept monetary authorities from using the money supply to manage the ups and downs of the economy. The world supply of gold at any one time is fixed, and the quantity cannot be quickly contracted or expanded as economic times require. When the economy was in recession or depression, it was difficult or impossible to rapidly expand the money supply (in this case, gold or silver) as a stimulus.

But the link between money supply and the economy has not proven to be consistent. There are many other factors aside from the quantity of money that determine the direction of the economy. Leaving the quantity of paper money in the hands of a central bank or in some cases politicians has not always led to a healthy economy, but to hyperinflation and economic crisis. This often brought about cries for a return to the use of gold as the only money instead of paper.

Bullion coins sell at a small premium to the metal. Gold bullion or gold minted into bullion coins is still advocated as partial security for an investment portfolio, especially in times of economic uncertainty or crisis. But gold is not a producing asset. It has no earnings. It pays no interest or dividends. Its value depends on the desire of others to have gold. Should fiat paper money trend toward losing its ability to perform the functions of money, gold or silver could replace some or most of paper money's utility.

This raises the question as to whether a gold or silver mining company common stock could also serve as a safe anchor for an investment portfolio rather than the actual metal or bullion coins. The shares of gold and silver companies may be classified as exploration, mining, or royalty. They may even be grouped in an exchange-traded fund for gold miners or even for junior or exploratory gold miners. The royalty companies receive metal royalties in exchange for advancing capital to the mining company.

Many shares of precious metal companies are listed for trade on the exchange and should bear some relationship to the price of the metal itself. In the fall of 2015, mining company shares were down 90 percent from their high a few years before, whereas the price of the metal was down only about 30 percent. Mining company stocks are more price-volatile than the gold and silver metal. Although there is a relationship between gold mining stocks and the price of gold, the relationship is not consistent. Mining stocks, as is true of all company shares traded, reflect future expectations of earnings. Consequently, as metal prices rise, so should mining share prices.

$ $

CHAPTER 38

$ $

Bonds

A bond is a promise to pay. It is a legal obligation. It promises to pay the principal amount at maturity or on call and to pay a specified additional amount—interest—regularly. The interest payment is stated as a percent of the principal and is usually paid in two parts-every six months. Typically, the bond principal amounts are $1,000 in the United States.

Bonds can even represent a promise to pay principal and interest in currencies other than the currency of the issuer's nation. A Japanese company could sell dollar bonds in the United States or Germany, promising to pay interest and principal in US dollars.

Of course, there is a market for all types of bonds. The original buyer does not have to hold them to maturity. And often, lots in size multiples of five bonds move more easily than a $1000, or single bond.

Bonds promise to pay interest, usually a fixed amount, twice every year until they are redeemed at maturity, when they return the promised principal. Sometimes they are called by the issuer for early redemption, repaying the principal and a bonus for early redemption. Bonds as an IOU make scheduled payments that are enforced by the legal system. Failure to pay as promised is a default. Not only is this a black eye on the issuer, but payments will be required by the court. If the issuing organization does not have the money to pay as promised, it in default. The court will control the assets—through a court-appointed interim administrator— until some settlement can be reached. This may even result in corporate liquidation by sale of all assets.

Bonds involve an interest-rate risk as well as a credit risk. Suppose Alice bought a newly issued 5 percent twenty-year bond for $1,012. The bond was issued with a $12 premium. Current rates on bonds of this risk and maturity were therefore yielding about 4.95 percent. Two years later, current rates for a similar eighteen-year 5 percent bonds of this credit risk were yielding 6 percent—a better yield. If Alice wanted to sell her old bond at this time, her 5 percent bond would have to compete with 6 percent bonds of her maturity. To yield 6 percent, the value of her bond would have to fall below $1,000, selling at a discount to, say, $895. Such is the influence of changing interest rates on price.

In fact, price and yield are inversely related. If bond prices rise, yields fall. If yields fall, prices of existing bonds rise. The interest payment is fixed for the life of the bond. This price fluctuation of existing bonds due to interest rate changes causes prices to change. The change in price reflects interest rate risk.

If Alice's bond had just one year to maturity, and we know $1,000 is expected to be paid in one year, it would not sell at such a big discount. The bond would only need to sell at about $990 to yield 6 percent ($10 gain plus $50 interest = income of $60, or 6 percent on the $1,000). The closer the bond is to maturity, the less the discount (or premium) on price. And it sells for little interest-rate risk.

As a bond investor, one way to protect against interest-rate risk is to build your bond portfolio with staggered maturities, sometimes called a *ladder*. Bonds are issued by business corporations, national governments, and lesser governments. In the United States, national bond issues are called *US Treasuries*, and those of lesser governments in the United States are called *municipals*.

US Treasuries are US legal obligations to pay interest and principal in US dollars by the government. Consequently, they have the highest credit rating. Bills (Treasury bills) are their shortest maturities—twenty-eight days, three months, six months, and so on—and therefore they have very little interest-rate risk. Bills do not pay interest but are sold at a discount to yield their return.

Treasury bonds (T-bonds) are most often issued with thirty-year maturities. TIPS are T-bonds that pay interest adjusted for inflation using the Consumer Price Index (CPI). Treasury notes are issued with anywhere from two- to ten-year maturities. Certain agencies of the US government also issue bonds.

The Treasuries are the most secure investment security in the world at this time. Many are held abroad. Treasury securities are heavily traded in the nonlisted or secondary market and are very liquid (easily bought and sold).

Municipals are debt obligations of states, cities, counties, school districts, and other political subdivisions of a state. Most are general obligations supported by the full taxing power of that government. Still, prospective investors need to learn about the taxing reliability of the issuer, tax receipts from taxes levied, and so on.

Some municipals are revenue bonds (not general obligation) that depend on a specific stream of income, not taxes. For example, a bridge may be built using bond sales to finance it, with bridge tolls dedicated to paying the interest promised and some set aside for meeting maturity payment. A revenue bond has no taxing capability to support it. Therefore, municipal revenue bonds have a higher credit risk and higher interest rates, and investors need to research a bond's prospects.

A great advantage of municipal bonds is that the income is free of the federal income tax, since the early days of the constitution preserving state rights. This allows municipal bonds to sell with lower interest rates than taxable bonds. A 5 percent sewer district bond could sell competitively with a 7 percent corporate bond for you, depending on your tax rate. The taxpayer may also escape state income tax, if the bond issuer is the state or within the taxing state.

Corporate bonds are also available to the investor. Their interest payments are taxable. Obviously, the credit risk or the quality of the bond varies widely. Standard & Poor's and Moody's rate these bonds on credit risk. Standard & Poor's investment-grade ratings for bonds are AAA, AA, A, or BAA. The interest rates they must pay depend on the quality rating. Lower-rated bonds will require higher interest rates of the issuing corporation to sell near par ($1,000). High-yield bonds are not investment-grade and are sometimes referred to as junk bonds. Some corporate bonds are traded on an exchange, and the rest are traded in a secondary market by investment dealers.

$ $

CHAPTER 47

$ $

Some Common Stock Investment Strategies

The title for this chapter uses the word *some* because there are far too many strategies for one to be expected to list them all.

One common investment strategy is called *contrarian*. This approach is to select shares of companies that most investors do not currently want. The belief is that shares of a company go through phases of popularity and lack of interest. Therefore, look for shares that are on sale because of lack of popularity. If the fundamentals of the company are good, buy it cheaper rather than when it is popular and higher in price.

The implication of a contrarian strategy is that you like the company and its prospects and want to be an owner, but you do not follow the herd by paying a high price. This approach can be applied to sectors as well as individual company shares. By sectors, we mean shares grouped by industry, such utilities, health care, and biotechnology.

Another approach to investing in common shares is called *buy and hold*. This may be used along with a contrarian approach, but the emphasis here is to invest in companies' shares that you will be happy to be an owner of for a long time, perhaps indefinitely. You have no plans to sell. An advantage here is that you can expect to generally be free from continuous managing of the investment. Still, you have to do your research.

Some investors want to depend on the compounding of dividend income. These investors look for companies with an established record of paying dividends and, ideally, a record of increasing dividends. These are

$ $
# CHAPTER 39
$ $
Futures

A *future* is a contract obligating the buyer to buy an asset (or the seller to sell an asset) at a specified future date and price. For the futures market to function, contracts are standardized so that the quantity and quality (if needed) are specified. Our purpose here is to define the term and use. Futures are not usually a part of most investors' portfolio.

Futures differ from options in that the option gives the owner the right to purchase or sell the asset, whereas the future contract obligates the owner to buy or sell the asset as a purchaser. Some futures contracts require physical delivery of the asset, while others are just settled in cash. Often ownership of a contract can just be ended at some point by selling any contract with the same date and price, closing the position. No one needs to handle physical delivery unless they wish it.

Futures contracts, or futures, are often used in commodities, currencies, and financial instruments. A farmer who wants to presell his harvest can get a fixed price ahead of harvest to eliminate the uncertainty of receipts. A currency contract can be used to secure a fixed price for an exporter who has sold equipment to a foreign buyer who pays later on product delivery. A financial institution that has agreed to provide a fixed-rate mortgage on a plant being built might hedge the risk of a change in interest rates by buying a future on a Treasury debt instrument.

Not only are futures an important risk hedge in many transactions, but speculators can also play an important role for the economy by shifting commodity supply. Farmers of spring-sown wheat harvest in late August or early September, can assure price of sale through a future contract.This tends to even out the supply and price of wheat over the year—a benefit to both farmers and consumers. Anyone can speculate on a commodity's price rising or falling by trading in futures contracts. Trading in futures requires the buyer and seller to put up a "good faith" dollar margin on entering into a futures contract.

Options on futures contracts are also traded and provide greater control for less money; in other words, more leverage. But this is an alternative usually for speculators, not investors. If an investor wishes to take a position in commodities or on Treasuries, a simpler way to proceed is through exchange-traded funds (ETFs). Some are commission-free, but not all. For example, IFI is an ETF holding three- to seven-year US Treasuries. (This is an example, not an investment recommendation.)

$ $

CHAPTER 40

$ $

Commodities

Holding a position in commodities provides control over a real asset. Commodities include oil, copper, natural gas, precious metals (such as gold), and agriculture (such as wheat and corn). Investment in commodities requires knowledge of such things as weather, planting cycles, regulation, world demand and supply, and so on. It requires a different approach than common stock, preferred stock, and bonds of industrials, utilities, transportation, communication businesses, and other assets.

You can use futures to hold a long or a short position, but as you may be limited in time periods and margin requirements, you would need to proceed carefully. If you hold the actual commodity, you have management concerns like storage and insurance to consider. Again, ETFs are likely the least troublesome way to invest in commodities. For example:

- CORN is an ETF for the commodity *corn.*
- WEAT is an ETF for the commodity *wheat.*
- SOYB is an ETF for the commodity *soybeans.*
- DBC is an ETF for a commodity index.

If you want to look for trends in an ETF or a commodity index, you can better visualize trend changes by computing a moving average. As presented before, to compute a fifty-day moving average, for example, average the closing prices for fifty days and then, for the next point, add the next day's price and drop the oldest price from the average. Each day, add in the newer price, dropping the oldest price from the average, and so on. A moving average hides some of the volatility of the prices.

$ $

CHAPTER 41

$ $

Real Estate

Real estate is real property—a real asset, like land and/or buildings. It does not include paper assets. An investor can buy and hold land and buildings. These usually are productive assets. That is, they yield an income. But of course, real estate fluctuates in value and sale price.

The income on land can be from leases for buildings and rent received. Farmland can be leased for dollar rent or a portion of the harvest. Single-family homes and multiunit dwellings can provide rental income. One can also invest in commercial and industrial buildings through a leasing arrangement.

Investment in a real estate investment trust (REIT) without having to act as a landlord is much more convenient for an investor. REITs trade in the stock market, adding liquidity to the real estate holding. REITs themselves pay no income tax as long as they distribute at least 90 percent of income to their shareholders, where it is taxed. The government taxes shareholders just as they do shareholder dividends from corporations.

Certainly, not all REITs are the same. Some may just hold debt instruments like mortgages, which are not real property. Others could be a basket of single family homes leased for rental income. Some may specialize as owners of the buildings and/or land for retail malls, commercial real estate, and even industrial land and/or buildings. It is important to learn the objectives and holdings of a REIT. For example, are retail land or buildings at risk as more retail spending is done by online shoppers?

Alternatively, an investor interested in real estate can seek exchange-traded funds (ETFs) that have portfolios of REITs, providing more diversification for the real estate investor. The diversified portfolio bundle may be spread over different regions of the country or even over several countries. But again, determine the nature of the underlying assets of the ETF to evaluate the risk.

Underlying assets may often change in value. If the real estate investments are restricted to a specific region, you may wish to determine the changes in values of real property. If the REIT holds mortgages, its value can depend on interest-rate changes as well as the risk of the value changes of the underlying real property.

PART SIX

Financial Management of Investments

$ $

CHAPTER 42

$ $

Allocation

A popular investing strategy is to allocate funds to various investment categories. The expectation is that such a distribution will provide less fluctuation in the value of the total investment principal, but offer a steady growth in value over time. The common categories for such a portfolio are common stock/equities, fixed income/debt obligations, short term/ money market debt, cash, and precious metals. The percentages in each category usually vary with time to retirement, risk tolerance, and the state of the economy.

Less volatility may allow the individual to ignore the day-to-day management of the portfolio. Equities(common stock, REITs and so on) can provide the expectation of growth in value of the portfolio while also some compounding of income through dividends. Fixed-income securities(bonds, mortgages) provide some stability of principal and allow compounding of the interest income. The money market investment provides a very liquid and stable, near cash reserve with dependable but lower returns.

The cash itself provides a backstop for emergency needs and a source for participation in unexpected investment opportunities and unforeseen emergencies. The gold (and/or other precious commodities) portion exists as a backstop in times of national economic crisis, such as hyperinflation, lack of confidence in the currency and/or financial institutions, and political instability.

As an example, let's consider two investors, John and Fred. John is thirty-seven, with a wife and three children in their teens and a middle-class income. Life insurance can provide family financial protection in the case of early death of one or both of the parents who provide the family income. But they do have to financially prepare for their college education if that need arises, and certainly eventual retirement support. John might choose the following allocation.

Equities (ETFs or investment companies)	60%
Bonds (as fixed income)	20%
Six-month certificates of deposit	10%
Cash	5%
Gold bullion coins	5 %
	100%

John's view is that the equities—the ETFs, and the investment companies—will be the most volatile, but they also provide the best opportunity for growth in value. With this allocation, he has no need to follow day-to-day fluctuations. Annual reports allow him to sleep nights yet provide progress toward his goals.

In contrast, Fred and his wife have children who have left their parents' home and are steering their own future. At age sixty, with ten years to expected retirement, Fred is looking for more stability in the value of his investments. In ten years, he wants to be able to begin drawing on funds to support a retirement lifestyle. He might look to an allocation as follows:

Equities (utilities and steady dividend payers)	20%
Bonds (municipals and investment-grade industrials)	60%
Mix of money market funds, cash, and precious metals, depending on the state of the economy,	20%
	100%

Allocation strategies call for rebalancing as the investment proportions deviate from the plan allocation. If John's equities grow to 75 percent of their allocation during a bull market, it is likely time to take some gains and distribute the funds to the other categories. This should bring the allocation back to the desired levels. This rebalancing has the advantage of selling equities when they have become expensive and buying them when they are cheaper.

$ $
# CHAPTER 43
$ $
Individual Retirement Accounts

The individual retirement account (IRA) is a federally authorized account that allows the owner to escape the federal income tax on the returns to the principal during its accumulation. This provides an incentive to save for retirement. There are two types of IRAs: a traditional and a Roth IRA. Each allows returns on the investment to accumulate without taxation, but you must not withdraw the funds accumulated during the accumulation period to avoid being taxed.

This can make a huge difference over time as the tax-free returns are reinvested. Recall our discussion in chapter 2 about compounding. Compounding returns each year, free of the income tax, allows accelerated growth in the account. The account will grow much faster with tax-free returns reinvested, increasing the size of the retirement fund.

The traditional IRA allows both a limited deduction annually from taxable income for contributions to an IRA and the compounding of returns during its life. You may begin taxable withdrawals at the age of 59.5 and are required to start withdrawing funds at the age of 70.5. Both the tax-deferred deposits into the IRA and the returns are free from federal tax until withdrawal. State income taxes customarily parallel the federal tax rules. Income taxes are imposed on the withdrawals.

For the Roth IRA, your deposits to the account are from income already taxed, but withdrawals are not taxed. There is no required minimum amount of payout required. You can start withdrawals after 5 years if older than 59.5. You could even leave withdrawal to your heirs.

Some choose to establish their IRA with a bank or credit union, using a savings account or certificate of deposit for their investment. Others may choose a self-directed account with a brokerage company. The self-directed broker account allows you to select your own investments within limits. You can select stocks, bonds, or even options.

A more fully self-directed account can allow real estate, small business, and precious metal investments, but excludes life insurance and collectables like wines, antiques, and cars. Any trading of assets within the IRA are not reported to the IRS and are not taxed.

As you approach retirement, you may have an accumulated 401(k) with the company or organization where you are employed. Employers often participate in building the fund with their contributions and, along with your contribution, may provide a sizeable component to your retirement kitty. You can move these into an IRA as you retire without incurring any tax liability until age 70.5. As you withdraw from this fund, you are going to have to pay income tax on the withdrawal. But you need not withdraw until you reach the age of 70.5. Then you must begin withdrawing at least the minimum required annually so that it can be taxed.

This age 70.5 required distribution is avoided in the Roth IRA. The fund's investment can be self-directed by you within limits, depending on the alternatives your financial institution provides.

$ $

CHAPTER 44

$ $

Investment Analysts and Newsletters

There exist many investment newsletters that seek to advise you on which common shares to buy. As such, they are usually required to register with the US Securities and Exchange Commission. Being registered does not mean controlled, certified, or approved. Some of these advisers tell you when to buy and what you should pay for a specific common stock or other investment. Some recommend trailing stops as principal (the amount invested) protection. A few even recommend when to sell.

The newsletters are interested in selling you a subscription to their letter for a fee. A few newsletters even charge fees amounting to as much as thousands of dollars per year. In most cases, they promote their advice by reporting their investment success or at least part of their investing experience. They may seek to establish their credibility by providing testimonials to their investing experience and/or cues to their system in selecting their recommendations.

I find the promotion of their newsletters usually lengthy, as they repeat their message many times as they bid for your business. And there are many of them. They may specialize in certain industries like gold stocks, mining stocks, or health stocks. A few will specialize in an investment strategy like current income rather than growth or appreciation.

We can also divide the analysts' newsletters into those based on either fundamental or technical analysis. The fundamental analyst's newsletter concentrates on seeking undervalued stocks or those whose value is expected to increase, usually because of revenue and profit forecasts. They work to find information they believe will lead to an increased price.

Technical analysts, on the other hand, make their recommendations based usually on share price patterns and volume behavior in the market. They believe their system identifies new trends or other patterns in the price of the stock. At least one makes recommendations based on data about buying by insiders. Insiders are usually officers and/or directors of the company accumulating or selling their company's stock. These insider transactions must be reported to the government, which periodically releases the information to the public.

The newsletter service can provide investing ideas, but there is usually little help on timing. While the common stock value recommendation may be useful, it may not fit for a one-year portfolio. Newsletters can recommend but usually provide no help as to how long one is expected to see some result by increased earnings or other causes for appreciation. This is, of course, very difficult to forecast. They may be most useful for an investor who can hold the investment indefinitely. Occasionally a target price is recommended. However, a recommendation based on yield by dividend income does not usually suffer from a timing issue.

The newsletters tend to follow a regular issue pattern—daily, weekly, or monthly. However, once committed to a publishing schedule, they find it necessary to provide a recommendation or story each issue, and perhaps they also review their past recommendations. They feel a need to provide news or a new recommendation each time, even if there is not much to tell their readers. It would be nice if they would grade their recommendations or skip an issue if they have nothing to say. Sometimes they fill in by promoting a companion newsletter.

In any case, newsletters cannot serve up an ideal investment all the time. They are not as perfect as they might wish you to believe.

$ $

CHAPTER 45

$ $

Investment Advisers

Some investment or financial advisers seek to provide comprehensive advice not just on stock portfolios but on all invested assets—often using an allocation model agreed upon with their clients. The client arrangements differ widely. In some, the client turns over the authority to execute decisions for all buying and selling of investments. In other cases, the adviser asks for approval from the client for each investment transaction.

In some cases, the adviser uses a mathematical program to build and rebalance the asset allocation. These are referred to as *robo advisers.*

Advisers usually give their advice for a fee based on the value of the assets, but the adviser fee depends on such things as how much management the adviser is asked to accept. The annual fee may be based on a percentage of the value of the managed investment portfolio, or it may be a flat dollar amount due each year. In other client relationships, the client manages the investments and just requests an audience with the adviser periodically to review the investment positions for an hourly fee.

The Investment Advisor Act of 1940 requires larger investment advisers as well as newsletter analysts to register and file with the US Securities and Exchange Commission (SEC) if they are managing or advising assets of $100 million or more. Depending on the nature of their clients, advisers managing or advising assets of less than $100 million may also choose to be registered investment advisors (RIA) and register with SEC. Regardless of size, investment advisers—whether a person or a firm—are not permitted to give advice that is fraudulent or deceitful. Also, they cannot enter into transactions between themselves and their clients, unless they have formal prior client written permission.

RIAs have a fiduciary responsibility to their clients. That means they must give suitable investment advice and act in the best interests of the clients. Any such government registration is not meant to endorse the adviser or provide any recommendation.

An individual or firm managing or advising $25 million assets or more, or operating in thirty or more states, is a federally covered advisor and is required to register and file annually with the SEC. Typically, any firm or adviser operating in a state or advising six or more clients in the state must register with the state.

Registration and/or filing of reports with the government does not consist of an endorsement. You need to make your own evaluation.

$ $

CHAPTER 46

$ $

Crisis Management

There can be times in an investor's life when the economy and financial markets are considered to be in crisis. Among these might be negative interest rates on bank savings and other accounts that could cause large withdrawals of cash from financial institutions. Most people are not anxious to pay financial institutions for holding their deposits. Large cash withdrawals might push the government to a digital, cashless economy. A panic run on banks by cash withdrawals from weakening financial institutions would force them to rely on Federal Deposit Insurance Corporation (FDIC) deposit insurance, but the FDIC has nowhere near the funds necessary to pay all accounts in the event of a country-wide banking collapse.

Another potential crisis would be the federal government's deficit spending, running up the Treasury debt beyond its ability to pay all the interest and bonds at maturity. The lack of confidence in paper currency might also bring about a crisis. Foreign holders of dollar deposits who wish to hold funds in other currencies could flood the dollar currency market, driving down the dollar's value relative to other currencies. A massive sale of foreign holdings of Treasury bonds for dollars in the Treasury market, followed by dumping of dollars in the currency market, would also constitute a crisis. The prices of imports could then skyrocket.

A collapse of security markets by both domestic and foreign owners of securities might bring tremendous losses in wealth. Prices of goods and services could rise so fast as to create hyperinflation. Should our credit system deflate like a punctured balloon, credit would disappear—no credit cards, no sales on credit.

Should one or more such events ever come about, you will likely not want to hold common stock or any securities. Any paper assets could and have registered great price declines in past history. You could find yourself not wanting to maintain dollar deposits in financial institutions. You may not want to hold currency in your household safe. Governments could be helpless in support.

Your best bet may be to hold real assets and not paper assets. Real assets are limited in quantity and cannot be multiplied by a printing press or other means. Look to houses, land, farms, precious metals, gems, jewelry, art, antiques, and even commodities, if they can be stored without deterioration. Among the most convenient may be gold or silver coins in denominations useful for the purchase of goods and services. These could become most useful in global currency wars, currency runs, lack of confidence in the currency or hyperinflation destroying paper currency claims.

Because precious metals are easily identified and are limited in amount, they are often held as asset reserves. But these precious metals are unproductive in themselves. They do not produce income. They are just there, and the price can go up and down.

The money supply in the United States has increased greatly from 2007 to 2015. Debt has increased sharply in recent years as well. Many millions are reported to be dependent on food stamps. Savings interest rates are near zero. Labor participation has fallen every year since 2007 and is the lowest since the 1970s, according to the US Department of Labor. In the not-too-distant future, the government may have trouble making the interest payment on its debt plus entitlements like Social Security and Medicare.

As of October 2016, the US dollar is the most acceptable global currency in the world. Management of the US dollar is a serious challenge to the Federal Reserve and the US Treasury. Rising US debt might eventually cause a lack of confidence in the dollar. The hope for trade and global economies has rested on the value of the US dollar and its acceptance in foreign trade and as foreign country government and individual reserves. But the international watchdog of currencies is the International Monetary Fund (IMF), not the US Treasury. The IMF could issue and manage a new global currency should the confidence in the US dollar collapse without a new acceptable currency to take its place.

mature companies usually in a stable business, where the nature of their business allows steady dividends. You then can arrange for automatic reinvestment of all dividends into shares of the same companies so that the number of shares and their dividends increase over time. This is compounding.

Other investors seek investments in companies that are reinvesting internally rather than those paying nothing or little of their profits in dividends. They pay little or no dividends, believing that an investment back into the company provides for growth in earnings and therefore stock price over time. They believe the rate of return on their investments inside the company will exceed the returns their shareholders can achieve with dividends outside the company. They believe they have better opportunities. Thus, the return to shareholders comes through increases in market value of shares.

Then there are those who believe they can find company stocks that sell for less than their value. They seek undervalued stocks, expecting that the investing market participants will later recognize the undervaluation and the market will revalue shares by pushing up the price. It was once argued that stock prices were always fully valued, given that all legally allowed information is publicly available. However, not all information really is available—certainly not behavioral information from investors. What investor behavioral information may be available is not available at all times. Little data on investor emotion can be found. Could information that does exist possibly be inferred by market behavior itself after the fact?

Technical market analysts believe that important company information shows in changes in the market price and volume data of the stock. Some, for example, observe market behavior by using a moving average of the stock price to erase random volatility, in order to identify the price trend and breakouts in the trend. Others look for unique market price patterns to reveal investor behavior. That is not to say that market price is only driven by human emotion or the mind, but those certainly contribute. Profit prospects can usually dominate price movements, but market price volatility can be blamed on changes in profit expectations, random shifts in supply and demand, and changes in the mind toward expected returns from assets.

CHAPTER 48

Conclusions

My objective in this stock market primer was to introduce you to investing and the stock market and to impress upon you the influence of human behavior on investment. In other words, human tendencies and emotions play an important role in the success or failure of your investment goals.

It is important to point out that humans are all selfish. The decisions they make are attempts to reach their own personal goals. Some of these selfish decisions are viewed by society as greedy. Those investment decisions are thought to be responses to the incentives visualized by the investor.

Among the less obvious behavior is the failure to recognize the money illusion, which accepts nominal returns rather than real returns. The investor accepts the dollar return as a positive return without identifying the loss in the value of the dollar due to price inflation or smaller packaging.

Introspection or mirror thinking leads investors to believe that others think the way they do. If that were really the case, then if you bought shares in X company because it was undervalued, everyone should come to the same conclusion. If that were the case, however, there should be no sellers of X company shares.

Another human error is the expectation that if the stock market has been rising—as noted by the Dow Industrial Average, the Nasdaq Index, or the Standard & Poor's 500—then it will likely rise tomorrow. This is the human tendency toward extrapolation. If Y company stock is rising today, the belief is that it will rise tomorrow. If its earnings rose in the last period, the odds are that it will rise next period. If real estate prices have been rising ten straight years, they will rise next year. That bias is only human and can be correct, but it is also not risk-free.

Loss aversion is another human reaction common to investors in the stock market. If investors face an unrealized loss in a stock or any asset, they do not want to accept it by realizing the loss though a sale. Investors tend to believe they were not wrong to select that stock and it will recover. Selling at a loss is an admission of failure. The careful use of stop-loss orders takes this emotion out of the selling decision.

Investors often have funds that are not invested—idle cash balances. These idle funds are not working. Often, that outlook leads to the desire to find something in which to invest. This usually results in lowering the standards of a good investment, and poor results follow. If investors follow that inclination to be fully invested, they may not have the cash ready for an opportunity that later arises.

Avoid following the herd. Your friends' and neighbors' enthusiasm for the stock market tinkers with your mind. When the market is moving in a negative direction—along with the attitude of your friends and neighbors—do you refuse to be influenced? If they are all positive, be sure to maintain your objective outlook. Be independent and objective. It's your money, not theirs.

Stock prices do fluctuate. No price stays constant. Volatility of shares changes over time. Many an investor views this fluctuation as centered around a "normal" value. This observation can lead to a normalcy bias. Even if share price is down, the belief is that it is moving about a normal value. But volatility changes for the market as a whole and for individual stocks over time. The belief that they have identified a normal price can result in unexpected losses when the range of movement changes.

Assume the price rose after purchase at $50 to a price of $55 and then $60. Each time, an investor would want to move the stop order up to partially protect the gain. Better yet, he could have entered a 10 percent trailing stop at $50. In that case, if it declined 10 percent, the automatic instruction would be to enter a stop order to sell. If, however, it rose to $60 a share, the trailing-stop price would move up automatically to protect some of the gain.

Some expectation about a particular share price's volatility can be learned from a share's beta. Often publicly available, a beta measures the volatility relative to the market. If beta is greater than 1, the share price fluctuation will accentuated; if less than 1, share price will move less than the market. The use of stop orders removes the emotion surrounding a normalcy bias. If you can set target prices for selling and use them, it takes the emotion out of selling decisions.

The contrarian approach seeks to incorporate at least some behavioral data of the mind. It seeks to identify investor behavioral mistakes, such as selling behavior pushing a share price or even the market too low (oversold) or too high (overbought). The technical analyst infers that certain price movements can be attributed to unidentified, underlying fundamental and/or behavioral changes.

Investors should approach the investment scene with a plan. Select an allocation plan for investments in various assets that provide a comfortable balance for risk. Do not gamble by putting 100 percent in the stock market. For your stock portion, do your research. Remember—it's your money, not your broker's, analyst's, or adviser's.

$ $
# ABOUT THE AUTHOR
$ $

Stephen Archer spent several years in the securities industry in Minneapolis and Seattle. He has also participated in seminars on Wall Street. But he was also a survivor of forty years of academic life, during which he authored many college finance textbooks, including *Portfolio Analysis* with Jack Francis.

He received a BA and MA in economics and a PhD in finance from the University of Minnesota. He is a past president of the Financial Management Association and treasurer of the American Institute of Decision Sciences. He was named Professional of the Year in Higher Education in 2011. He was founder of the finance department at the University of Washington, founder of the internationally recognized *Journal of Financial and Quantitative Analysis*, and founder of the generic MBA program at Willamette University.

He is a retired Certified Financial Planner, and his many published papers include studies on the earnings-dividend relationship, inflation's impact on stock values, and diversification for risk reduction in portfolios. He has lectured in Canada, Italy, England, Switzerland, and Japan. He was a Fulbright Scholar and a postdoctoral Ford Foundation Fellow at UCLA in mathematics and statistics.

Printed in the United States
By Bookmasters